January 2016. To Gerry,
From Mam & Dad with Love –
xx

A Delicate Wildness

THE LIFE AND LOVES OF

David Thomson

1914–1988

To Peter and Anne, my parents

A Delicate Wildness

THE LIFE AND LOVES OF
David Thomson
1914–1988

JULIAN VIGNOLES

THE LILLIPUT PRESS
DUBLIN

First published 2014 by
THE LILLIPUT PRESS
62–63 Sitric Road, Arbour Hill,
Dublin 7, Ireland
www.lilliputpress.ie

A CIP record for this title is available
from The British Library.

10 9 8 7 6 5 4 3 2 1

ISBN 978 1 84351 633 0

Set in 12 pt on 15.7 pt Perpetua by Marsha Swan
Printed in Navarre, Spain, by GraphyCems

Contents

Acknowledgments

This book is based on David Thomson's writings, notebooks and correspondence, and on the recollections of family and friends. All his published works have an autobiographical element, so I have made much reference to them throughout. He also had a great archival sense throughout his life, keeping large amounts of notes and letters.

There were many people who encouraged and helped with this project and to whom I'm grateful. I had very valuable guidance at crucial stages of the work from Tim Lehane; Joe Duffy gave me great advice on draft chapters; Timothy, Luke and Ben Thomson were supportive and candid in recollection of their parents; Sally Harrower and her colleagues at the National Library of Scotland, Edinburgh, afforded me a most pleasant time, as did the Rathmines Library in Dublin. Angela Bourke shared Thomson insights. Seán and Desmond Biddulph and Steve Bober were invaluable because of interest in their own family histories. I'm grateful to Joe Mulholland and RTÉ Archives for the interview he recorded with David Thomson in 1987.

I've shared a love for all matters *Woodbrook* with my friends, the owners of Woodbrook House since 1970, Mai and the late John A. Malone, who always celebrated their home's literary heritage and had a great welcome, allowing me to photograph the house and grounds. Others helped along the way: Kate Kavanagh, Luke Dodd, May Moran, Marion Dolan, David Gillespie, Lionel

Gallagher, Mary O'Rourke (née Pogue), Percy Carty, Neil Belton, Stina Greaker, Ríonach Uí Ógáin, Evelyn Conlon, Dave McHugh, Norman Colin, Judy Cameron, Melanie and Patrick Cuming, David and Sue Gentleman, Christopher Ashe, Cathal Goan, Bairbre Ní Fhloinn, Diane Barker, Patrick Kinsella and Jeananne Crowley. Tim Dee was an incisive guide to BBC matters and on David's legacy. Marie, Michael, Christopher and Catherine Heaney and Faber and Faber Ltd kindly gave permission to quote from Seamus Heaney's work.

My wife, Carol, and sons Eoghan and Rory, encouraged me from the start. Antony Farrell of The Lilliput Press was enthusiastic when I approached him about telling the Thomson story, and both he and Fiona Dunne proved exacting editors.

This book would not have been possible without the support and generosity of the late Martina Thomson, who talked to me at length, even as her health began to fail. I had phoned her from the famous Henry's pub in Cootehall in May 2013 during that year's John McGahern Seminar, in which David's twenty-fifth anniversary was marked. I asked what she would think about my writing his biography. Her response was positive and the journey began.

Introduction

On the evening of 26 February 1989, a group of distinguished Irish people gathered in The Royal Irish Academy in Dublin for a commemoration. They were to honour not a fellow Irish person, but a Scotsman, born in India. It was one year after his death. He was David Thomson – writer, folklorist, radio producer, scholar and honorary Irishman. He suffered sometimes-frail health and poor eyesight, but had a mind quietly on overdrive for most of his life.

Seamus Heaney began proceedings that night: 'This is a wake of sorts, where we remember the care, delicacy, research and affection that David invested in this country – as a historian, a folklorist and as a person. He had made intimates of his readers.'

Jim Delaney of University College, Dublin, paid tribute to Thomson as a folklore collector and co-author of *The Leaping Hare*. 'He was scholarly and not just a folklorist, but a literary artist' he said. The poet Nuala Ní Dhomhnaill said that in *The People of the Sea* Thomson had carried with him what she described as 'the mind-set of the Irish language so totally', though he never learnt the language and was apologetic for that.

The broadcaster Seán Mac Réamoinn said of Thomson's most famous work, *Woodbrook*: 'I know of no book that explains us better to the world outside. And does so with such unsentimental sympathy.' He continued: 'That seemingly remote and withdrawn man had this vivid and acute knowledge of people and things and what people were doing, what things were significant in the world. He was his own man, but he was also *our man*.'

John McGahern also recalled *Woodbrook*: 'It is strange in the English tradition of writing about Ireland. I know of no voice like it; there is no savage indignation, no exasperated tolerance, no dehumanizing farce, and no superior tone. It has a rare sweetness and gentleness.'

I first came across David Thomson when browsing in Fred Hanna's Dublin bookshop during the summer of 1985. I saw the hardback edition of *Woodbrook* in a remainder sale. The jacket photo was an atmospheric shot of water and reeds. Something struck me about it and I bought it. It changed my life. And so devastated was I with the ending, that I immediately read the whole book again.

I was working in RTÉ Radio, so I responded by making a documentary to express my admiration for the book. The programme, 'The Story of Woodbrook', was a labour of love. When, about a year later, I got to meet David himself, I was face to face with a hero, a Dylanesque figure, who engrossed me in a way no one had ever done.

This book is the first to tell the David Thomson story; the complexity of one gifted man's life; the trials and triumphs of his interaction with the world; his wit and wisdom; his take on love and loss – and his frailties. It's an account of his journey as a writer and an appraisal of the work he left us. Perhaps most of all it's a story about the people he loved and the people who loved him.

David Thomson's legacy of thirteen published works were developed out of the notebooks, the ones that usually filled his jacket pockets, containing thoughts, reflections, sometimes inspired ramblings. These were compiled in the corridors of the BBC, in pubs, on park benches in North London, in the company of literati and the homeless.

In relation to Ireland, he illuminated the role of folk memory in our understanding the past. He shone a light on our history and was an important chronicler of the fortunes of the Anglo-Irish community in the mid twentieth century.

And what of David Thomson, the man? He came from a family that flew a flag when they were in residence, where as a visitor after Newton house in Nairn had been converted to a hotel, he was refused entry because of his appearance. Once, a child on a London street insisted that David take a sixpence the boy was offering him. He was an Oxford graduate who became an Irish farmer. He once had a love affair with a woman who worked in an African brothel.

He liked having a drink with homeless people in London. His greatest work concerns a love story with a girl who was only twelve, but who haunted him romantically and creatively. He liked to brush against women's hair on buses. He wrote a heartfelt letter to Harold Wilson protesting about the Vietnam War. He identified horses by their names in photographs. He admitted that animals sexually aroused him. He once wrote an angry letter to complain about a ban on men shaving in the borough of Camden's public toilets. His death in 1988 caused his wife an extended period of profound grief.

In his published work and in his notebooks, Thomson not only shows literary prowess but reveals himself openly and frankly to his readers. His writing enriches us with curiosity about many aspects of humanity – tradition, belief, memory and love. His writing expresses one man's yearning for contentment as he deals imaginatively and articulately with the urges and passions that drive all of us. He was flirtatious, bold, playful, bohemian, and eccentric, with 'the manners of a king, the gentleness of a saint', according to one of his sons. Seamus Heaney summed up his spirit when he said David had 'a delicate wildness'.

In May 2013 I was involved with John Kenny of University College Galway and Philip Delamere, County Leitrim's arts officer, in organizing a tribute to David Thomson on the twenty-fifth anniversary of his death, as part of the John McGahern International Seminar. *Woodbrook* admirers emerged, many with their well-worn original editions, their enthusiasm palpable.

I travelled to Nairn in the Scottish Highlands, by train as he had done many times, to visit his childhood home. I saw the fisher town that he described – now with no fishing vessels to be seen, but pleasure yachts bobbing in the breeze. I crossed the bridge over the Nairn River, where his ashes had been scattered, to a the beach where British troops prepared for the Normandy landings as David began his career at the BBC. At Newton, the family seat to which David Thomson felt mixed allegiances, a gardener worked in the grounds overlooking the Firth of Moray; looking up at the bare flagpole that once used to announce the family's presence, he remarked that their era was well and truly gone now. But the change that concerned him more was climatic, as the flower bulbs he was planting might be 'fooled' by the mild winter days and sprout but are killed by spring frost. David Thomson loved flowers and would have approved of this concern.

One day last winter, as I drove slowly down the lane that was once the Woodbrook avenue, towards the house and past the places he described so beautifully, the memory of Thomson's words, written about this corner of Ireland so long ago, came dramatically to light.

I realized again why I wanted to write a book about him.

David, aged ten, with pets including Kuti the dog, at Pattison Road, Hampstead, May 1924.

The Spring

In memoriam David Thomson

Choose one set of tracks and track a hare
Until the prints stop, just like that, in snow.
End of line. Smooth drifts. Where did he go?

Back on her tracks, of course, and took a spring
Yards off to the side; clean break; no scent or sign.
She landed in her form and then ate snow.

(Which is why Pliny thought the fur goes white
And why one friend imagined the Holy Ghost
As a great white hare on the summit of a ride –

Then sprung himself at last, still weaving, dodging,
Haring it out until the very end,
The shake-the-heart, the dew-hammer, the far-eyed.)

Seamus Heaney

Martina Thomson's Diary

12 October 1988 Nairn

The river was fast and brown with choppy waves. I tore the seal off the plastic bag. There was the stuff. It was not so soft as I had imagined it, but hard like little gravel. I took a handful of ashes and put it in my hair. Then I took the bag to the edge of the river and strewed the remainder into the fast flowing water. It left a white trail, which travelled at great speed down the river. I rubbed the ashes into my hair, I felt you could spare that bit.

By the time I was back to the hotel bedroom I thought of those ashes as mingling with the open sea of the Moray Firth.

A Delicate Wildness

THE LIFE AND LOVES OF

David Thomson

1914–1988

1. Nairn in Darkness

'All the Irish should be hanged!' said Granny in a louder voice than usual. She was known to everyone as kind and gentle.

This fragment of a breakfast-table conversation, recounted in *Nairn in Darkness and Light*, echoed through David Thomson's life, and with it the fraught relationship between the two islands. He remembered it as a seven-year-old from a morning when his household in Nairn was discussing the impending arrival of David Lloyd George, the British prime minister, to holiday in the Highlands that summer of 1921.

But David's grandmother was asked to clarify her remark; did she mean to include the family's local acquaintances in Nairn, the O'Toole's? That family was related to Saint Laurence O'Toole, the twelfth-century Abbot of Glendalough and Archbishop of Dublin, some of whose descendants in this part of Scotland had decided, in order to disguise their Irish background, to change their name to Hall, after Ireland's Easter Rebellion of 1916. Granma stood firm.

Far away from this town in the north-east of Scotland David Thomson's life had begun, five thousand feet above sea level, in the city of Quetta, then part of British-occupied India. His father, Alexander Guthrie Thomson, a Scottish native born in 1873, had obtained his commission into the Indian army as a 2nd lieutenant in 1893. His posting was with the 5th Regiment of Punjab Infantry founded in 1849. The regiment later became part of the army of the new state of West Pakistan in 1947, and Quetta, close to the Afghan border, is now part of the Punjab region of Pakistan. The two Pakistan states were created, controversially, as part of the Indian independence settlement in 1947, in the two regions of India that had Muslim majorities.

The Indian army had been established for the colonial purpose of subduing a subcontinent, controlling its warring factions and maintaining it as part of the British empire. There were different wars during the eighteenth and nineteenth centuries; uprisings by Sikhs and Muslims, then the Mutiny of 1858, which nearly ended British rule. The Indian army's rank and file largely consisted of Indian men, as Britain and Ireland alone could not have supplied the army manpower needed for a country of India's size. At the time Alec Thomson got his commission in 1893, the ratio of Indian to British servicemen was two to one.

When Thomson had graduated from Sandhurst, he ironically couldn't afford to remain in the British army itself. Officers at that time needed a separate income if they were to live the 'appropriate' life, to be 'like well-off gentlemen'. For the privilege of being officers, the men had to buy their own uniforms, day-to-day and ornate ceremonial ones, as well as swords for battle and state occasions. The Thomsons were well-to-do, but the Finlays, the family he would marry into, were in a different league financially and in terms of connections. Why there was no 'dig out' by the wealthier side of the family at the Newton estate in Nairn for the young Thomson is unclear. But India was perhaps attractive on its own merits. The Indian army, which was usually short of officers, provided everything free. Also, in India, infantry officers were mounted, and that appealed to Alec Thomson. India was an adventure for men like him. The polo was apparently better, too.

The Indian army maintained British power in the subcontinent by at times benign, but mostly firm and sometimes brutal means. It carried out a notorious massacre in April 1919 at Jallianwala Bagh, in the city of Amritsar, opening fire on a crowd protesting at the arrest of local leaders. Exact figures for casualties are disputed but hundreds of peaceful protestors, including children, were mown down. Ninety-four years later, in 2013, David Cameron became the first British prime minister to visit the site and offer apologies, describing it as a 'deeply shameful event in British history'.

David's father, Colonel Alexander (Alec) Thomson, and mother, Annie Finlay Thomson (courtesy Steve Bober).

As the young Alec Thomson began his military career stationed in British Baluchistan, where Quetta is located, he was thinking of someone back home in Scotland. Before he'd left, Thomson had fallen in love with Annie Finlay, his first cousin, when she was aged just fifteen. She was born in 1880. When they became engaged during one of his home leaves, her family, on both sides, disapproved. The Episcopal Church of Scotland had only just changed its rules to allow marriage between cousins.

Annie Finlay managed to follow her fiancé to India, chaperoned by her aunt May, whose husband was in the Indian Civil Service. She married Alexander Thomson on Christmas Eve, 1907. The newly-wed Annie was to move from her native Scottish Highlands to a very different and exotic mountainous region of the world.

A contemporary account describes one aspect of life for women in the Raj, as British-administered India was known.

> The honey smell of the fuzz-buzz flowers, of thorn trees in the sun, and the smell of open drains and urine, of coconut oil on shining black human hair, of mustard cooking oil and the blue smoke from cow dung used as fuel; it was a smell redolent of the sun, more alive and vivid than anything in the West.*

In the late nineteenth century, thousands of young men left Britain for India to serve as administrators, soldiers and businessmen. Many young women followed in search of marriage – and even love. These young women were known as 'The Fishing Fleet'. They endured discomforts and monotony, but also

---

* Anne De Courcy, *The Fishing Fleet – Husband Hunting in the Raj* (Weidenfeld & Nicolson Ltd, London, 2012).

found an intoxicating environment, the sky aflame with vivid colours, pungent scents from, to them, exotic shrubs and flowers.

The Indian sub-continent Alexander Thomson and his family were to leave behind in 1914 was about to experience a great upheaval. In 1915, one of that country's great sons, Mahatma Ghandi, returned from Europe to his enormous native country to champion the Indian masses and begin his unique independence struggle, based on civil disobedience.

David Thomson's sisters, Mary and Joan, were born into this colonial environment in 1908 and 1911. Their only brother, David Robert Alexander, to give David his full name, was born on 17 February 1914. A third daughter, Barbara, was born later in Surrey and a fifth child, Lily, died in infancy in England. Stephen Bober, David's sister Barbara's son and David's nephew, recalls his mother speaking of her father as a kind and just man, driven by the best sort of Christian values.

Alexander Thomson's regiment, the 58th Vaughan Rifles, was active in France during World War I. He was decorated with several medals – some for service in particular campaigns, but he also received a Distinguished Service Medal and the French Croix-de-Guerre. Philip Mason in his book on the Indian army, writes of gallantry and devotion to duty, and at one point refers to 'clearing a German trench' to describe a much more brutal activity, almost casually describing the loss of life involved. He recounts a particular engagement involving Thomson's battalion. Sir Arthur Wauchope of the Black Watch saw his regiment's flank exposed, but the 58th came to their aid: 'And a fine sight it was to see the 58th pushing forward, driving all before them. A year's experience has taught our men that there was no regiment that ever served in the brigade they would as soon have as the 58th to come to their aid.'*

Alexander Thomson was seriously wounded at Rue-du-Bois on 9 May 1915. He was mentioned in dispatches on 31 May 1915, 'for gallant and distinguished services in the field'. He returned to England where he lay for weeks, his body mutilated, in a darkened room, as his wife nursed him, between May and September 1915. He recovered and returned to the army, rising to the rank of Lieutenant Colonel in October 1919. He retired in May 1920. The family then lived mostly in Buxton, Derbyshire, and he 'commuted' by train for years

* Philip Mason, *A Matter of Honour – An Account of the Indian Army, Its Officers and Men* (Jonathan Cape, London, 1974).

to Manchester to different jobs. One of these was managing a factory, which employed disabled soldiers. Later he became secretary of the Hampstead Garden Suburb Trust. This was a far-sighted early-twentieth-century progressive town-planning project to create a model community in this part of north London, with people of all classes living together in 'beautiful houses set in a verdant landscape'. By 1935 the Suburb comprised a large swath of about 800 acres stretching from Golders Green in the south to East Finchley in the north.

In the winter of 1914, David's mother left India with her two daughters and her nine-month-old son. It was a long voyage on a troop ship bound for France. Since secrecy prevailed after war was declared in August that year, his mother had no idea where her husband had been ordered to go, except that it was to the front. Alexander Thomson, not yet thirty, acting undoubtedly with personal bravery, carried out his duty, which involved willingly ordering other young men to almost certain death, as his wife nursed their only son, an infant who in time would quietly reject all of his father's military values.

Annie Thomson brought the baby David and his sisters to her mother's house, Tigh-na-Rosan, in the town of Nairn, the home of David's Granma – she of the 'hanging' remark. A short walk away was Newton, the large family seat owned by Annie's brother, Robert Bannatyne Finlay. The house was later converted to a hotel, and frequented by, among others, Charlie Chaplin, who holidayed there several times in his later years during the 1970s. Robert Bannatyne Finlay, later Viscount Finlay, had bought the house in 1887 during the first period he was MP for the area, the Inverness Burghs, between 1885 and 1892. The hotel still has Finlay and Chaplin suites.

David's maternal Granma's home, Tigh-na-Rosan in Nairn, as it is today.

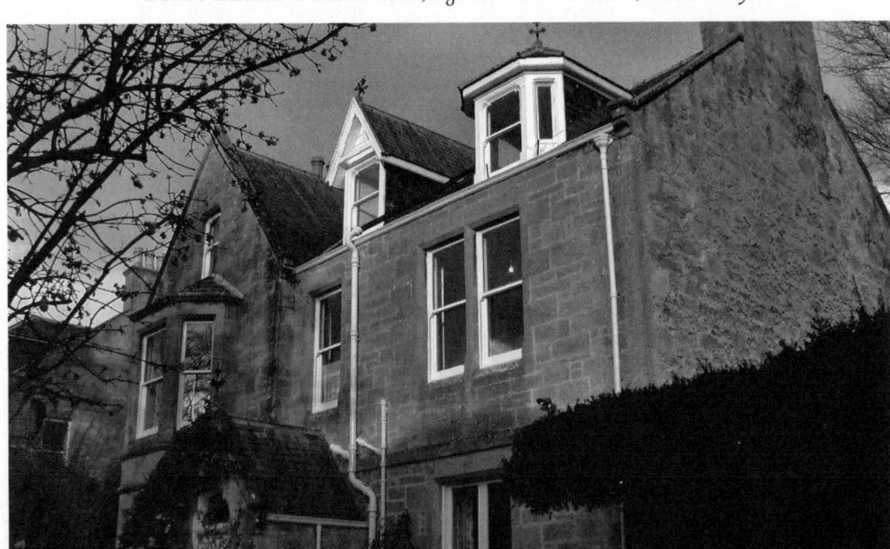

Newton House, Nairn, in the Scottish Highlands, David's uncle Robert Finlay's family seat, now a hotel.

For the young David Thomson, his maternal grandmother's house and his uncle's mansion in Nairn, on the Moray Firth north-east of Inverness, became his most formative home as he began a lifelong relationship with that town, its history and traditions. In *Nairn in Darkness and Light* (published in 1987, a year before his death), he returned to the place of his childhood in this last published work. It's an example of the Thomson blend of autobiography, memoir and evocation of place, in this case the world seen through a child's eye via the prism of the seventy-two-year-old writer. The book earned him The McVitie's Prize of Scottish Writer of the Year in 1987.

In *Nairn in Darkness and Light*'s opening chapter he continues to evoke that summer of 1921 and Lloyd George's visit. At Newton disapproval is expressed at the Prime Minister's apparent intention to reach a treaty with Ireland, giving it a degree of independence. The treaty negotiations, which were to have long lasting consequences for both islands, had begun in London that summer. The household in this privileged part of Nairn had its own local preoccupations, as David recalls a little sarcastically: 'At breakfast and in the conservatory and billiard room the men were usually talking and laughing. Was the wind too strong, would the grouse fly high? Was the sun too bright for fish to rise, had the rain made the golf course greens too soft and slow, the tennis courts too quaggy?'

It could be said there was anti-Home Rule form in the house: Robert Finlay had under William Gladstone's influence initially supported Home Rule for Ireland, before 'turning coat' on that issue and leaving Gladstone's Liberal Party. He had now risen to the inner circle in the government of Lloyd George. Between 1916 and 1919, Finlay was Lord Chancellor in Lloyd George's coalition government, then replaced by Lord Birkenhead, who was later a negotiator and a signatory of the Anglo-Irish Treaty. In 1921, Uncle Robert, as David Thomson refers to him, was appointed to the Permanent Court of International Justice, established by the newly formed League of Nations, and which became the International Court of Justice in 1946.

That summer Robert Finlay and the family were shocked by the idea that Éamon de Valera might succeed in detaching Ireland from the British Empire to form a republic that would include its Protestant minority, who were hostile to the idea. This Protestant minority and their declining fortunes would later be a crucial experience in David Thomson's life and part of the inspiration for *Woodbrook*.

When Lloyd George went fishing that autumn not far from Nairn, he not only offended the unionist consensus, but committed a fishing no-no; while others in his party were using flies – unsuccessfully – on the Kerry River, the Welshman slipped away downstream and apparently attached a worm to his line and landed a twenty-ounce brown trout, the only catch of the day, 'Thereby adding to his sins in all the eyes of Newton, where fishing with a worm was taboo.'

Thomson's evocation of that time ends as he notes that a letter arrived to interrupt the British leader's holiday, from de Valera in Dublin, and Lloyd George had to convene a Cabinet meeting in nearby Inverness.

David said in 1987 that he began to write, 'as soon as he could read and write'. At the age of seven he won a literary prize, that same year, 1921, in a magazine called *'Little Folks'*. The prize was a modest one: a framed photograph of Derwent Water in the Lake District. He recalled taking the bus to the nearest town to their home in Buxton, Derbyshire, to collect his prize. He was dying to show his trophy to his sisters, but sat on it by mistake on the bus home and the glass splintered on the picture, so that was what his siblings saw. The story itself was about flower show daffodils that go missing from his uncle's garden, and a boy and his brother's attempts to retrieve them.

Nairn in Darkness and Light opens with a letter from David to Kolya Yakovlevich, a childhood friend who like David, spent summers in Nairn. Kolya had a Ukrainian father but his mother Catriona was Scottish, a Ferguson. She had met Ivan Yakovlevich while they were both studying medicine in Edinburgh University. They fell in love, got married and went to live in Kiev. Things didn't work out though David never found out why, but Catriona returned to Scotland with Kolya, or Kolly, as he became known. He was regarded as a delinquent, a little mad and engaged in shoplifting, but David admired him, it would seem, for this 'whiff of sulphur' about him, not to mention his good looks and natural charm. David's grandmother thought the child should have been sent to Borstal, after a particular incident where he damaged the roof of her house, and rain caused a ceiling to collapse, wrecking of a valuable Persian inlaid escritoire.

David saw Kolya every summer till he was seventeen, their mothers being tennis partners. It was on long cycling excursions with the Ukrainian–Scottish lad that Thomson's lifelong love of the countryside first developed. Their letter-writing forms one of the threads of *Nairn in Darkness and Light*. He refers to Kolya as his cousin, but says he was never sure whether he was a real cousin or not, leaving a riddle that might possibly have involved a transgression by a member of the family at some stage.

There are strong hints in the young Thomson's letter writing to Kolya of his future talent. In one, he's describing morning prayers in Newton and regretting that his friend wasn't there to enjoy this scene with him:

> I was kneeling beside uncle Tom and you would have been beside me and he was muttering his usual cross things all through the beginning and if they hear they take no notice but today they did because when uncle Robert got to the Lord's Prayer uncle Tom said, 'No Popery' quite out loud, and some of the new maids giggled. Cathy and Gina I guess, and Uncle Robert stopped and Mrs Waddell marched the maids out of the dining room but it should have been Uncle Tom who was marched out.

Thomson later admits embellishing this 'No Popery' scene, but of course he was recognizing the value of doing that. He then sums up the climate in Nairn and evokes a memory many from these latitudes would share:

> It often rained in Nairn for days and days, but I think most people's memories of childhood summers live in blue skies, white clouds, the dust of the roads, the earthquake cracks in sun baked pathways, the blue and white sea, green leaves and grass, hot pebbles and the yellowy whites of the sea sand. Mine certainly does.

David aged nine, with his parents, sister Barbara and Granma, at Newton, August 1923.

David had a morbid curiosity, aroused by one of the employees, the henwife at Newton, as she went about her work. The birds' feeding time first attracted this curiosity, and then attention turned to a darker matter. The children, David and his three sisters, disliked the woman because she was 'ostentatiously cruel'. He says she killed hens slowly, relishing, he believed, in the agony of her victims. Then he makes an admission. He sought to witness the killing secretly – by design, rather than accident: 'For the sight and sounds aroused an emotional tension in me that was at once both repellent and attractive. I would think about it in bed with sorrow and compassion for the bird and yet I would long for the day when I would be old enough to kill one with my bare hands.'

When the family weren't in Nairn, they lived in Derbyshire and later at Hampstead, London. David was sent to a succession of schools between the ages of five and eleven. He disliked them all. There was one in Buckinghamshire he hated so much he named it Dotheboys Hall, as he was reading Dickens's *Nicholas Nickleby* at the time and thinking of the gruff and violent Wackford Squeers of the novel. He noted that it was the days before private schools like his were subject to inspection. The couple who ran 'Dotheboys Hall' (he doesn't reveal its real name) punished with punches and kicks and resorted, he says, to starvation – their favourite. A friend of his, Ian Gordon, was locked up for a week, he recalls, because he could not learn by heart the words of the Sermon on the Mount. When David's parents found out they moved him to University College School in London. It was here that a seemingly harmless incident occurred that had a profound effect on the rest of his life. 'I remember every detail of that November day during my second year at University College School and of the sleepless night that followed.'

Even with his already poor eyesight, he had attempted to play rugby. Although he says he had strong thighs and could play as a forward, his poor eyesight meant that the ball was invisible for much of the time and the other players were 'blurred like white ghosts'. During the game that day, he received an accidental kick from someone on his own team just at the side of his right eye. The first result was confusion at Geography class the next day, when a simple exercise in map reading became a problem. His eyes began to be inhabited by shapes and blobs that reminded him of protozoa, the organisms visible when viewing tissue through a microscope.

When his mother brought him to a specialist, a Dr Burnford in Wimpole Street in London, we get a fascinating glimpse of his mother's emotional life as much as we do of his eye condition. Dr Burnford had, David's mother said, 'saved her life' when treating her husband, David's father, during the war. The doctor had changed his name from Bernstein to assimilate better in the post-war period in England. He had become, according to her son, a close friend of Annie Finlay Thomson: 'His sense of humour was something like my mother's which must have been one reason for her fondness for him, that deep affection which amounted, I now believe, to love.'

Thomson leaves that fascinating thread there. But it's typical of his willingness to explore emotional matters in his writing. A consultation with another doctor, Mr Maclehose, followed. He maintained that the kick to the head was not necessarily the cause of the haemorrhage behind the eyes, but it may have hastened it. His prescription was drastic for the young David: he was to lie in a darkened room for at least six weeks. His parents read to him during this time. A man came daily from a school for the blind in Great Portland Street to teach him Braille.

The rest of the 'cure' was then revealed to him. He describes his mother's anguish at not knowing which of the prohibitions were worse to a boy of eleven. He had to give up reading and writing entirely until he stopped growing – at twenty-one. He was never to exert himself, lift heavy objects, never to play games, not 'even cricket'. Running and diving were out, and if he dropped something, he had to feel for it with his hand and avoid looking at the floor. All this was designed, according to the medical knowledge at the time, to prevent the revival of the protozoa in David's eyes.

Tim Dee, from a later generation of BBC radio producers than David, in a talk he gave on BBC Radio 3, referred to this early period of David Thomson's life using the image of the floaters that crossed David's vision as a metaphor. He became a kind of human floater, Dee says, passionately concerned with the stories of the people he recorded or lived among, 'but also as someone who was somewhere else, who focused those stories through the prism of his own sensibility. The floater is both a separation from and a colouration of what the eye sees. And so, brilliantly, David Thomson, saw, lived and wrote.' *

In 1925 David's parents made what he himself agrees was a wise decision. They sent him to live in Nairn with his grandmother, 'which benefited me for the rest of my life'. They wisely predicted, he concludes, that doom would beset him in London, if he was unable to do all the things his friends were involved in, that he'd 'have to hide when the gang came to take me on an evening's rampage'. It's possible also that David's parents were aware of mental fragility at this stage in his life. Martina Thomson reflected on this in 2013, believing that it showed a vigilance regarding their son's welfare.

David describes in detail the train journey that began this great wrench. He had made it before but always had the comfort of having his family with him, as he had on so many previous journeys to Scotland. It was the 19.30 night train from Platform 13 at Euston. His father had hired him a pillow and blanket at the station. Thomson likes detail; the train needed two engines to haul the carriages up the Camden embankment, passing the street that would be his future home, its construction an aspect of rail engineering history that Thomson would explore many years later in *In Camden Town*.

As morning broke and Scotland approached, the train thinned out as carriages were detached and the remaining cars joined the Highland Line at Perth, where David describes a surreal encounter – with sexual overtone – as he returned the hired pillow and blanket to a larger-than-life girl who collected them on the platform:

* *Archipelago*, Winter 2012.

–Twas a braw nicht, I'm thinking, but ye were on your lonesome?

–Aye

–Well now, you're a canny loon, or look to be. Next time ye travel north, send word for Meg o' Perth an she'll go south to bring you. Mind my name well now. Meg. They all know Meg. And Meg will share your pillow wi' ye and we will travel couthie warm togither.

She laughed and pushed her barrow further up the train.

He learnt the names by heart of the stations from Perth to Nairn, 'like a poem in my head, Dunkeld, Dalguise, Ballinluig, Pilochry'. He and his sisters could recite them: Killiecrankie, Blair Atholl, Struan, Dalnaspidal, and the highest place where a board said 'SUMMIT'. He remembered his sister Barbara had once made strangers laugh by shouting, 'There's another station called Gentlemen.' A branch line then cut through the Cairngorms with more stops such as Dumphail, Forres, Brodie, Auldearn and then Nairn. This line didn't survive the cuts of the 1960s and the present route to Nairn goes through Inverness and takes the line to Aberdeen, leaving the stations of Thomson's childhood as much a part of history as Jacobite rebellions.

The young David arrived in Nairn to a not uncommon discord with an elderly relative. In his case it was his maternal grandmother. Apart from her view of the rebellious Irish, he says she had kind and gentle qualities, but David and she seemed to share a mutual antagonism. After the three years he lived with her, he could only recall acerbity. He speculates that her husband's early death caused her spirits to sink so low, 'they were lost to her entirely, buried deep in her unconscious mind as a protection against pain. I cannot remember ever hearing her use my Christian name in the vocative once during those three years.'

The person who kept the tension between David and his grandmother from getting out of hand was her daughter Margery, his aunt. He describes how 'the invisible wire that joined Granma and me' became so taut that it threatened to break. It needed someone to slacken it. David was drawn to Margery anyway because she was a writer and he was curious about the hut, complete with a large German typewriter, she used in the grounds of Tigh-na-Rosan for her work. Margery Walker (née Finlay) had worked for Lord Rhonnda, the minister for food during the First World War, who administered rationing between 1917 and 1918. David's teenage observation of her writing career and his reflection on it in *Nairn* shows the writer's urge in him. He laments her bad luck when her book, biographical essays about people who had made a mark in health policy, *Pioneers of Public Health,* had its march stolen, it seems, by a similar publication with a somewhat more engrossing title, *The Microbe Hunters* – a lesson for David, a salutary tale of winning and losing in publishing that perhaps stayed with him.

David believed that Margery's preoccupation with her book and fear of dying before she could finish it, kept his aunt aloof from that taut wire of enmity between him and his mother's mother. As he details this breakdown in the relationship with Granma, which he admits he was part of, he pleads that he was more tolerant of her than she of him. The enmity began over how well he washed dung off his hands before dinner and his use of salt: 'Great quarrels are born of great issues; possession of land, possession of woman, the dividing up of inherited jewellery. Ours was born of a pinch of salt and a speck of cow dung.'

There was a massive flare-up, followed by a solitary solution by the young Thomson, one that would be repeated years later after an emotional trauma in County Roscommon and remembered in *Woodbrook*: he took to his bicycle. It was a joyful, elemental ride in the snow through the dark where he felt he was free and proud. He was alone with his thoughts and the snow: 'Even jagged rocks were round and white and the strands of barbed wire above the stone dykes were dotted with blobs instead of spikes: the rectangular tops of the posts that held them were cushions; the thorns of whin bushes were shielded, the blackthorn's blackness was invisible, its thorns blunted.'

For each of the three years David lived in Nairn, the rest of the family holidayed there in the summers. He describes a particular break in the lonely autumn and winter months that came with a visit by his mother to check on the progress of his eye treatment. It's a description of upper-class Victorian sternness struggling with the inevitable warmth of a mother-son relationship, as he recounts her overnight stay. David was being kept for his own good in the darkness that gives the book its title. He longed for his mother in these lonely times of sensory deprivation – longed to feel her face and hands. One of these mornings when he know there was light outside that he could not share, he heard the door opening and it was her:

> I recognized my mother by her smell. I could not believe it but I knew it was she. She came running on her toes to me like a long leafy branch of syringa blown towards me by the wind, the delicate green leaves ... She did not speak. I could not. We stayed a long time like that, my hand in hers.

David is torn; he really wants to have his mother there, but he's not sure what they'll do together. There's anguish in his writing. He knows she will disappear from his life again for months, so he's not sure how close he really wants to get to her now. At one stage of her visit he even feels bored, ashamed to feel this way, but relieved when she goes downstairs again after they take tea together. The scene becomes an interesting meditation on the meaning of human closeness. His mind was telling him she'd be gone soon, so he felt a sense that he couldn't really savour her presence. Yet when she does go, he feels horribly alone. For her part, she is restraining her emotion. 'When the moment came her eyes, close to mine, shone with tears that did not escape but her voice was soft and steady. After she had closed the door silently behind her as she had slowly walked towards it, silently, I felt nothing. My heart was dead.'

During these years David questioned his family and their emotional and social behaviour. He becomes drawn to the more humble family of Sandwood Farm just west of Newton, only to be softly rebuked by them one afternoon and reminded that he was the nephew of a lord and the son of a colonel. He nevertheless contrasts this family with his own, praising the way he observes them always saying what they mean. But the family had a reverence for his grandmother, 'Mrs Finlay', that he couldn't unhinge. He cycles back to Newton from this encounter 'like an outcast'.

The stables (beloved of David Thomson) at Newton House, as they are today.

This day he had tried to cross class lines began and ended, however, with a completely different experience. As he returned to Newton by the servants' entrance, he saw Shetland ponies gathered by a fence. David then put into practice something a local man had shown him earlier that day when he found David in the cold with no hat or gloves. 'One of them stood eating with its hindquarters to the fence. I slid my cold fingers under its tail and feeling about found it to be a mare. It felt warm, but it was not only the relief from cold that pleased me.'

The theme of sexual awakening is a frequent motif in memoir writing. Thomson treats this in his lyrical way. It takes the form of a long dream sequence involving Jeannie, a local girl and a journey they make together in a pony and trap, probably David's favourite form of transport. They meet in town and go on a jaunt where sexuality is tentatively explored. They risk her getting pregnant, as they think, by kissing. David pays as much attention to the horse's behaviour as he does to Jeannie's. Boy, girl and horse are in a semi-erotic cascade through fog and into summer sun somewhere on an empty road in northern Scotland.

> Jeannie leant close to me as we came through the fog, silent and clutching my arm, but when we emerged from it into the bright summer, she looked at me happily as though nothing had broken our journey. When we came to the grassy place Tweedledum [the horse] tried to go on to it, but seeing a wider, greener stretch ahead, I would not let him.
>
> – Let him, said Jeannie, he wants to piddle. Nein, Dum, if you wish to leave the room you hold up … and as he was doing it, she whispered to me.
>
> – It splashes on his legs if he does it on the road. That's why he held out so long. How about you? I've wet my knickers.

Martina Thomson knew about another substantial passage in this dream sequence in *Nairn*. She advised David not to include it in the finished manuscript and he reluctantly took her advice. We don't know what the writing contained except that it was sexually explicit, by the standards of the 1980s at least. It is the only part of David Thomson's papers in the National Library of Scotland that is unavailable, though catalogued.

Nairn has another notable admission. David confesses to being sexually aroused by animals, particularly horses. He describes the view of buttocks, udders, hips and tails, 'all of which aroused the unruly member, as Rabelais called it'.

The feelings he had for girls like Jeannie and for horses are mixed up in his imagination. He longed to comb Jeannie's hair as he combed one of the family's horses, Flossie. Tweedledum aroused in him a secret and forbidden emotion he says that he didn't understand till he was about sixteen, when a girl he knew took off her clothes and stood in front of him naked. The shape of her body bore for him a welcome resemblance to a horse's hindquarters. A girl's body from the waist down is similarly shaped, he observes.

> I hid from others the sensual, often sexual pleasure animals gave me – sight, touch, and smell. I have known some who like the smell of pigs and nanny goats that smell faintly, like ewes. Billy goats to me emit a powerful smell which disgusts most people, but is to me nostalgic and homely. Even stroking a cat may be regarded by strict Presbyterians as a carnal sin.

But Thomson follows this by introducing an intellectual dimension to the evoking of these primitive urges. 'The pleasure or revulsion we feel at the sight or touch of animals – the arousal of our deeply hidden instincts – may be just what makes animal symbolism in church, religious ritual and in myth, so powerful and universal.'

And he hadn't, it seems, put himself completely out on a limb with this revelation. The canon of the Episcopal Church, before his confirmation, urged him not to 'waste his seed'. A local laird, Alexander Brodie of Brodie, had written in his journal three centuries earlier: 'In going about the fields, I found the heart apt to rise with carnal delights in fields, grass, woods. This I desired the Lord to guard me against.'

He made another great discovery. The Battle of Culloden was fought on the moor between Inverness and Nairn, on 16 April 1746. The result changed the course of British and European history. It was here that the Jacobite army fought to reclaim the throne of Britain from the Hanoverians for a Stuart king. The British army was equally determined to stop this happening. France was involved on the Jacobite side, giving the conflict a European dimension. The ferocious war had come to Scotland – dividing families and setting clan against clan. Cumberland, the twenty-five-year-old general on the government side,was camped in Nairn overnight. Prince Charles Edward Stuart led the Jacobite forces and camped at Inverness. After a failed surprise attack during the night, his subordinates pleaded with him to retreat. But he ordered an attack. The battle lasted less than an hour, before the Jacobites fled, leaving heavy casualties. David recalls how he used to imagine the battle when his family went for picnics on the moor. His father had shown him the position of the armies, the horses and wagons, the soldiers, their weapons and their dress: 'It was vivid in my mind and once I had burst into tears as I read of the Jacobites' defeat. But at school I had learned nothing of it or any other battle except the date and the superiority of the English.'

This pursuit of knowledge and exploration of imagination runs throughout *Nairn in Darkness and Light*, from local references in Robbie Burns's poetry to the lives of Scottish lairds. David's intellectual journey delivered a very positive family side-effect when his curiosity about Scottish history unexpectedly caused a rapprochement with Granma. He had been reading and also listening to local lore about earlier times in the Highlands – getting his first sense of its importance, too. 'I was able to tell her details about the Battle of Culloden and its aftermath that astonished her. She began to listen to me and ask me questions, as though I was no longer a boy she had to put up with.'

David with his sisters; Joan and Mary, rear, Barbara, front (courtesy Steve Bober).

This had followed what David called 'the greatest blessing bestowed on him by his parents'. In the summer of 1926, when he was twelve, they bought him a small Corona typewriter. By the end of that summer he had learned to type so well he had begun his first novel. It was set at Culloden. He tested the story on his sisters by asking them to read passages out to him and suggest corrections. They weren't too impressed. But the twelve-year-old Thomson's mind was clearly thriving and producing, because a year later the book had become 'too large for anyone on earth to read'.

And by the end of the book, a maturing David is beginning to gently cast off the values of his family background. He is drawn to the Labour leader Ramsay McDonald and to the apparent, pre-Stalinist, socialist ideals of the Soviet Union. He took lessons in Gaelic, something he felt his father was silently deriding. 'I was also beginning to believe in pacifism, that it is better to submit to an enemy rather than to fight, which must have seemed to him a denial of his own career.'

This was probably the start of the break with his father, at least it signalled the retreat of Colonel Thomson's influence in his life. Many years later, Seamus Heaney, looking back on those early years as the writer had recalled them in *Nairn*, identified what he saw as David Thomson's humanity as a writer: 'Eye injury did not diminish his inner imagining eye, and the amphibiousness he then developed between the stern and kindly regime of high Edwardian family life and the impulsive, erotically charged freedoms of the natural world, prefigured the capacity he would later manifest as a writer, true to the inner and outer realities of experience.'*

Aged fourteen, David left the care of his Scottish family in 1928 and was enrolled in the progressive King Alfred School in Golders Green on the edge of Hampstead Heath. It was founded in 1898 by a group of parents who believed in the radical idea, that boys and girls should be educated together in a secular environment that encouraged learning for its own sake. The school wanted to provide an education that focused on what was best for the whole child; on the development of character and individuality.

According to John Russell, the school head between 1901 and 1920, its ethos was to 'help train up its scholars in the way of the good life, to help to fit them for effective work in the world, for effective sympathy and for effective joy'. Here, the delicate young Thomson was cared for educationally and emotionally.

* *The Sunday Tribune*, February 1989.

His inability to engage in physical activity was not seen as a disability.

In notes dated 3 September 1928, his first term in King Alfred's, he tackles punctuation; 'allow one space after a colon or semi-colon'. He types an example from Samuel Johnson: 'Small debts are like small shot; they rattle on every side and can scarcely be escaped without a wound; great debts are like cannon; loud noise but little danger.'

In another school notebook that survives, labelled 'A Survey of English Life and Literature', the teenage Thomson shows more than an average flair for his subject. In the opening page, 'Periods and their Characteristics', he asks, 'Can a general epithet justifiably be attached to an age or century?' He lists some well-known names and the year of their deaths; Browning 1889; Gladstone 1898; Ruskin 1900: 'They seem to mark the end of an era, but things are always in a process of transition.' Perhaps inspired by his English teacher, a Miss Hibberd, he wrote a comparison and contrast between Charles Dickens and William Thackery.

> They presented the Victorian world, lived in the same society, but saw it differently. Thackery had been an historian, Dickens an actor. Thackery safe-guards virtue by understatement. Dickens enjoys his villains, and has an unconcealed relish for life that Thackery hadn't. But Thackery came through much harder trials, and was also susceptible to extremes of depression.

Many years later, David wrote in a diary that he fell in love with the novelist George Eliot when he was sixteen and exploring literature in that school. There's also an untitled manuscript from this time, an incomplete novel, set on a Scottish moor. It begins, not surprisingly, with non-human characters:

> Her father was a chestnut, her mother of a dullish yellow hue, and she, well I might say, a mixture of the two. Nobody except her mother wanted her; and in fact, only the day before, Mr. Ross had told a friend that he had given up breeding all ponies but Shetlands. But there she was, a round bundle of soft hair with a head somewhere and four legs somewhere else, but all hidden in the long purple heather ...

Thomson, because of his clearly academic ability, which in a school like this would have been a badge of honour and, despite his sense of fun and mischief, achieved the coveted position of head boy before he completed his time in King Alfred School. He played Malvolio, Shakespeare's puritan 'party pooper' character, in a school production of *Twelfth Night*.

In 1931 he enrolled in modern history in Lincoln College, Oxford. The course began with the year 1495 and ended at 1914, the year of his birth. He was conflicted in his approach to the study of history: 'Historians are supposed to be impartial,' he wrote later in *Woodbrook*, 'but no one can be.' He came to believe during his university years that it was impossible to write unemotionally about Anglo-Irish history.

David had chosen as his special subject the British Commonwealth, 1649 – 1660, the era of Oliver Cromwell. When David came to County Roscommon the following year for the first time, not only did he hear the infamous name mentioned shortly after he arrived, he says, but he sought out as much information as he could about Cromwell's Irish exploits. This was an early encounter for him with the power of folk memory; he observed that Cromwell spread destruction widely but many violent acts attributed to him were done before he was born or while he was two or three years old. He discovered that 'The Curse of Cromwell on you' was still a common form of malediction in the early years of the twentieth century.

Something else was germinating in his mind at that time, a more contemporary political sensibility. David joined a society called the October Club for a time, a communist organization. There were many like him in those years from privileged backgrounds that embraced communism, partly in many cases as a reaction to their parents' values. David said in 1987: 'I didn't really take an interest in politics, not a close one. I had emotions about it rather than an interest.' During David's time at Oxford, a motion carried at the Oxford Union Debating Society caused a ripple: 'I would not fight for King and Country.' The passing of this resolution was seen as highly treasonous and there was even an attempt to reverse the decision by Winston Churchill's son, Randolph. David and his friends were in favour of the motion. David Thomson had in his own quiet way rejected the establishment he had come from, the movers and shakers of his ancestry, the great house of Newton and the imperial mindset of his family.

While at Oxford, he began taking odd jobs as a tutor. One of these, which began in 1932, brought about a fateful meeting with someone who became a central character in both his emotional and literary life, Phoebe Kirkwood. The relationship would be celebrated many years later in *Woodbrook*. The Kirkwoods were an Anglo-Irish family with both a London home at 22 Queen's Grove, St John's Wood, and an Irish estate in County Roscommon.

Between 1932 and 1943 David travelled back and forth to Ireland many times, employed as tutor and later as a farmhand, fell in love, got to know County Roscommon intimately and became a confidant of the Kirkwood family as their fortunes declined. David in these Irish years greatly developed his antenna for tradition, the heritage of his adopted part of Roscommon and the value of its folk history. He brought this sensibility to his broadcasting and writing career, seeking connections with the past both there and in his native Scotland. This discernment and fascination for ordinary peoples' lives, gained in the fishertown and farms of Nairn and on the Plains of Boyle, would stand him in good stead.

But in the summer of 1932, his relationship with Ireland was about to begin.

David, aged sixteen, with family dog (courtesy Martina Thomson).

2. Woodbrook: Enchantment in Roscommon

David was approaching sixty years of age as he worked on his memoir in Camden Town, recalling his first summer in County Roscommon, over forty years previously. He was remembering, in sensual tones, how he fell in love:

> I had to grasp her arms and lift her in. My hands must have sometimes been warm by then from resting on the sun-blistered paintwork of the boat, but I can remember distinctly how cold and wet her skin was at my first touch and how in a second or two the warmth of her body came through.

The 'her' in the passage is Phoebe Kirkwood. The relationship blossomed after he made the journey from London with her, her mother Ivy and her younger sister, Tony, travelling on by train from Broadstone in Dublin, to countryside totally new to him, but which he would celebrate in a special way. This period of his life became the setting for his most famous work, *Woodbrook* published over forty years after that summer, in 1974. As he would do later in *Nairn in Darkness and Light*, he was returning late in life to tell another story of his youth; or perhaps, more accurately, telling a story of love, growing up and understanding the past, set in those early years. Enchantment is one of *Woodbrook*'s themes; that simple piece of boating experience becomes a sense of wonder between man and woman.

Other features of the book reward the reader. One is the strong suggestion that events in the present and events centuries before in the same place are not really separated at all. Thomson senses that events like the Penal Laws and their effects still live in the soul of the area. Another aspect of time and its meaning is contained in a small detail of the pace of Woodbrook life, where the local postman would sometimes actually wait while a letter he was delivering was replied to.

Woodbrook was an estate about three miles from Carrick-on-Shannon on the road to Boyle. The Kirkwood family were planters from Cromwellian times, but of modest means, unlike their near neighbours the King-Harmons of Rockingham, whose estate was more than 30,000 acres. Geographically, Woodbrook House and estate were in County Roscommon, though the nearest town of Carrick-on-Shannon is in County Leitrim.

While at Oxford, David had been recommended as a tutor to the family by Anne Finlay, a cousin on his mother's side, who at that time was teaching painting to Phoebe, the elder child, in their London home in St John's Wood. It was a fateful introduction that led to the great love affair, which became central to *Woodbrook*.

Woodbrook House, photographed in the 1930s. Note the wings, demolished in the 1950s (courtesy Mai Malone).

Major Charles (Charlie) Kirkwood (courtesy Carrick-on-Shannon Golf Club).

Like David's father, his new employer, Major Charles Kirkwood, had been an officer in the Indian army and the two men knew each other when stationed in Quetta. Charlie Kirkwood's young wife was born Ivy Muriel Burton, in Brighton, in 1894. She had been an aspiring pianist and singer, something she resumed in later life. Her father, another army officer, introduced Ivy to Charlie Kirkwood in India. She had been sent there reluctantly in 1912 when she was eighteen in the hope of finding a husband. She married Charlie Kirkwood in 1915. David Thomson portrays her as a very strong presence in the household. In the letters that survive from the time, Ivy treats David almost as a brother.

The Woodbrook estate Charlie and Ivy inherited had a sporting claim to fame. In the early twentieth century, Charlie Kirkwood's uncle, Colonel Tom Kirkwood, ran a successful racing stables on the lands. Woodbrook, one of its horses, won the English Grand National in 1881. But its most famous progeny was The White Knight, who won the Ascot Gold Cup in 1907 and 1908.

The book is a panorama – part memoir, part love story and part historical narrative. Its great power is lyrical writing, where Thomson weaves the extraordinary out of the ordinary. He paints with words, as a realist, an impressionist and even as a surrealist. In his writing, the Shannon and its tributary near Woodbrook, the Boyle River, become like mythic waterways, the lakes and islands fascinating other worlds of light and half-light, the fabric of this often under-praised countryside a source of enchantment. The tone is set on page one:

> I was eighteen when I first saw Woodbrook. The children excitedly pulled me towards the right hand window of the car and I saw its slate roof from the turn of the road at the top of Hughestown Hill. It was midday and sunny. The slates shone for a moment between the leaves of beech trees and we descended rattling towards the house, looking out from the window of this old Fiat, which had fetched us from the station three miles away.

At the end of the first page, Thomson strikes a quite different note, one that resonates through the whole book. He had studied history in Oxford, but now he was about to experience a whole new outlook on the subject: 'I found in the days and years that followed that I had begun to uncover a physical past, which lives in my memory now where the details academically learnt have sunk.'

We're barely into the chapter when a hint of the darker side of the Woodbrook story emerges, reminiscent of the sentiment in his grandmother's casual remark in 1921. Thomson reveals that the Maxwell brothers, Jimmy and Tommy, from a local family who worked for Major Kirkwood, 'secretly cherished hatred for the Major ... whom, in day-to-day relationships, they loved – cherished this hatred because of his ancestors and theirs, and because it might help their advancement'.

Bridge Street, Carrick-on-Shannon, about 1940.

David Thomson, centre, working at Woodbrook in 1940. (Courtesy Desmond Biddulph)

David writes that the Kirkwoods were living their lives knowing little about the 'horrid legacy we had all inherited'. This early observation in the book shows Thomson's humanity, as he casts this Anglo-Irish family as innocent products of history. The once brutal landlord class of legend had been reduced to a mid-twentieth-century representative in this part of Ireland – the gentle, benign Charlie Kirkwood.

The Maxwells thought Major Kirkwood odd because he liked to paint, an abnormality for a man, in their view, which they put down to shellshock. David admits his surprise when he hears them speak harshly of England and English rule of Ireland. This is the 'eye opener' aspect of the book, Thomson confessing ignorance of the brutality of English colonial policy towards Ireland, a result of his education up to then, he concludes. His recalled also his own father's characterization of Ireland's Easter Rebellion of 1916 as 'stabbing England in the back'.

But this is only one thread. *Woodbrook* constantly changes course, one of its characteristics. History, strife and incident move aside, and the love affair returns to the centre of the narrative. It's a boy–girl story told lyrically, but scored with erotic undertone. This Roscommon rhapsody has carefully judged ambiguity and understatement at its core – partly relating to an undercurrent of age difference. David had fallen in love with Phoebe; he was eighteen and she, his pupil, eleven. But in revealing love for someone as young as Phoebe was, Thomson was being consistent with his direct approach to emotional and sexual matters, and perhaps also challenging the reader to accept the idea of this relationship.

> She was wearing light jodhpurs and a sleeveless shirt, the one I liked her best in at that time, the one I always think of as the strawberry shirt, not only because of its colour, but because the material was puckered into small pointed sections rounded at the base, each with a fleck of yellow in it, like a segment of a strawberry. In sunlight the colour glowed faintly on her cheek. It had a round neck rather low, no collar, no buttons. It left the whole of her shoulders bare, except a piece two inches wide, and was close and fragile enough to show the full outline of her growing breasts. It made her seem more like a woman than a child. Perhaps that is why I liked her strawberry shirt.

The fact that this passage is written about a girl who hasn't yet reached her twelfth birthday would certainly raise eyebrows nowadays. David's relationship with Phoebe has over the years been described as an 'innocent love affair'. But there's very little innocent about appreciating her 'growing breasts' or liking a garment because it made her 'seem more like a woman than a child'. But Thomson is casting moral conformity aside, in a way, asserting human nature artistically – that a boy or man of eighteen can see a pre-teen girl in sexual terms. He is also being honest, reminding us also, perhaps, of the ambiguity that surrounds sex and attraction.

Seamus Heaney once wrote that *Woodbrook* is 'a book that was at once an erotic idyll and a work of historical reconstruction'. In comparing it with an earlier work, *The People of the Sea,* he describes Thomson's art as 'the world regarded through an artfully innocent eye, one that thereby revealed all the more lucidly rights and wrongs, hurts and beauties, usually taken for granted'.*

The sexual energy is always tempered by a different evocation – a romance for the countryside, the changing light, the sounds and the texture of life on the estate, or that primal sensation as his hand held hers, helping her into the boat. Thomson weaves a scene around the syringa, or lilac, which he describes having become entwined with a more exotic, dark-leaf shrub that a Kirkwood ancestor had brought from foreign parts. The plants' intertwining becomes a metaphor for his relationship with Phoebe. There's a charge in the air, as David had removed his shirt to gather eggs in:

* Introduction to *The People of the Sea* (Canongate Classics, London, 2001).

Phoebe Kirkwood, in her early teens. The photograph was found by John Malone in the Woodbrook stables some years after he bought the property in 1970 (courtesy Mai Malone).

> As she took the flowers from me, she looked at my eyes and then pressed the flowers to her face. I kissed her shoulder and drew her against my naked chest, slightly and only for a second. She looked at me again for only a second when I took my grasping arm away and her eyes had changed. They were like open windows. She could never draw the blinds.

Her bedroom and his were separated only by a very light partition. So they were always aware of each other's movements, tantalizingly so, he implies.

> Both rooms looked westwards … towards the water meadow. The corncrake had begun its evening croaking hidden in the long grass there – 'crake-crake-crake-crake, crake-crake' – a monotonous and seemingly endless rhythm on one note which I have never heard anywhere but Woodbrook. It fills me with nostalgia now for the seething life of that house and it reminds me of the evening of syringa.

Ivy Kirkwood intervened to put an end to this liaison, and Phoebe and David's 'separation', as he refers to it in the book, began. Ivy said very little, but the message was clear: David and Phoebe becoming in any way physically intimate was not on. Tutoring had to be conducted on separate chairs, for starters. Phoebe also made a confidential promise to her mother, he tells us in the book, but doesn't reveal its detail.

This edict gives an extra tension and charge to the remainder of *Woodbrook*, particularly in a passage such as the evocative train journey he and Phoebe made that October to Ballinasloe Horse Fair, in a windowless railcar, with its hint of Thomson's equine fondness, too.

> We spent some parts of the journey laughing helplessly. But all the incidents were spaced between long periods of happy calm suspension during which we seldom spoke and had no thoughts, unless sensations count as thoughts – the rhythmic rocking and its soporific sound, the sweet wet smell of the October country air that came wafting through the box to mingle with the smell of horses that was so homely and ordinary to us.

Then there are the scholarly aspects of the book. Thomson delves forensically into the history of the area, weaving meticulous research and local lore. He tells the story of Úna Bhán, the subject of the tragic Irish love poem set on an island on Lough Key, close to Woodbrook. The legend goes that Úna McDermott fell in love with the son of a rival family, Thomas Costello. Following a combination of misfortune and misunderstanding, she dies of a broken heart without her beloved near her. They were then reunited in death and buried beside each other on Trinity Island. According to legend, trees grew on each of the graves and became intertwined. David relates the spirit of this story to himself and Phoebe.

> When I was happy with Phoebe I came across for the first time the stories of Tristan and Iseult, Deirdre and Naoise, and Abélard and Héloise. Together we read *Romeo and Juliet* and heard from country people the tragedy of Úna Bhán. In each of these stories there is a jealous parent, usually the father of the girl.

David Thomson experienced another form of jealousy. Other young men were attracted to Phoebe for the qualities of grace and beauty that Thomson describes. After graduating from Oxford, with no career in sight, David took on new private pupils for income. One of these, Tony Trevor-Roper, was invited by the Kirkwoods and David to come to Ireland one summer. When Trevor-Roper became fond of Phoebe, now sixteen, David said he became more jealous than he had ever been in his life. The fact that he couldn't join in the tennis and ping-pong that the others enjoyed made it all the more frustrating. Sporting activity was a problem for David because, having poor eyesight, he lacked the necessary agility. This exclusion caused something of a depression that Ivy Kirkwood, at least, seemed aware of. David wanted to leave Woodbrook forever. She encouraged him to take his bicycle and travel to the west of Ireland. He describes an odyssey, first travelling to Donegal, then to Connemara, all the time tormented by thoughts of Phoebe. He describes a lorry driver who brought him to his home in Kindrum in County Donegal, where he shared a bed with the man's three sons. They talked themselves to sleep in Irish, a language he'd never heard before, and he felt lonelier than ever as his journey continued.

Then Thomson pauses that whole narrative, to turn to history. With his great attention to detail, he traces the events of 'The Year of the French', 1798, when a force sent by Napoleon and commanded by General Humbert landed in Killala, County Mayo. The magistrate in the town was a Captain William Kirkwood, a distant relative of David's employer. Thomson's traces the unfolding events, the turmoil, the clash of cultures between the French and their Irish allies, and Kirkwood's fate to be caught in the middle. Carrick-on-Shannon was later the scene of a gruesome 'lottery', as the French and Irish forces were routed. A couple of hundred prisoners had each to pick a piece of paper; if 'death' was written on the piece they picked, they were immediately hanged at the door of the courthouse.

In his epilogue, David Thomson reflects on the 1798 Rebellion and other failed uprisings against English rule in Ireland and concludes: 'It is as though the whole of Anglo-Irish history has been boiled down and its dregs thrown out, leaving their poisonous concentrate on these six counties.' Thomson managed to steer clear of any categorization of his historical perspective – he's neither nationalistic or 'revisionist', but argues that great injustice was done to Ireland, without in any way suggesting that the legacy justified modern-day violent republicanism.

Idyllic life with the Kirkwoods was coming to an end by the early 1940s, as their fortunes declined further and further into debt. The happiest last years on the estate coincided with Europe's descent into brutal war. The family remained all year in Ireland because of the Blitz. Thomson writes about his feelings towards the war; he was naturally a pacifist, but at the same time believed that fascism was a great evil and seemed to reluctantly accept that its defeat could only come from war. He confesses that while friends of his had joined anti-Franco forces, he did nothing. He seldom read newspapers and when he did he was 'either bored or plunged into despair'.

He captures local ambivalence towards England. Tommy Maxwell came to him one day at the time of the Fall of Dunkirk as he was working in the fields to say that 'England is finished' and that 'Hitler had taken France'. The shock of this news sparked patriotism in Thomson that, he says, he thought was long discarded – since the age of fourteen when he had given up Scottish nationalism. News travelled slowly then and the radio was crackly and batteries were primitive. Charlie Kirkwood didn't comment much, despite his military background, or maybe because of the memory of it. David said he hoped that neither he nor his own father would be called up. In the winter of 1940, however, David did return to London to enlist and was refused, apparently on eyesight grounds. He returned to farming in Roscommon. A pastoral scene is revealed in photographs of this period that survive, showing Thomson and local men ploughing and preparing seed potatoes. The ploughing photo has another Thomson touch – the horses are identified and named by him on the back of each picture, giving them 'equal billing' with the humans, some of whose names he forgets.

David on cart drawn by the horse Carnaby (Desmond Biddulph).

Splitting seed potatoes at Woodbrook, 1940. Left to right; David Thomson, Jimmy Maxwell, Joe Fryer, 'one of the Muldoons', Tommy Maxwell (Desmond Biddulph).

The Kirkwoods' debts were by this stage crippling. Thomson mentions that at the beginning of the war, they owed the publican and grocer in Carrick, John Lowe, £500, a large sum in those days. The final option was to sell their treasured estate, the same fate many other gentry families were to meet. *Woodbrook* themes of time, memory and light return when Phoebe, her mother and sister are leaving Woodbrook for good:

> Charlie drove off jerkily and an arm waved. It may have been hers, but her coat and Ivy's were almost the same colour and the one window of the car that would open gave room for only one arm. The sun was dazzling on the snow. A few minutes later I watched the car climb Hughestown Hill and disappear.

David describes an incident the following spring. One night he left the house to tend to some lambs in a nearby paddock. When he lost his way in a completely familiar setting he puts it down to night blindness, part of his poor eyesight. But Willie Maxwell viewed it in a more mysterious way. Some fields were known to have 'a stray' in them, where if you got lost, as many had, you had to 'turn your coat inside out and walk across a river and you'd come back to your eye-sight'. David concludes that most beliefs of that sort are parables. He decided he must turn himself inside out because since the Kirkwoods had left, he still hadn't made a decision about his future.

David and Phoebe met again later in 1943 when the family were living in Kilmacanogue, County Wicklow. The Kirkwoods were related by marriage to the Jameson distilling family, Charlie's brother Billy having married Grace Helen Sara Jameson, so Charlie, Ivy and the family spent several years during the mid-1940s living in that family's properties at Howth Head, Sutton and Kilmacanogue. David describes his and Phoebe's reunion and walk to the lily pond on the Jameson estate where they 'spoke like strangers that want to get to know each other but dare not'. They sat on a stone seat and Thomson is elemental once more: 'The birds that sang were close together and more numerous, judging by the sound, than those we were used to hearing at Woodbrook, whose song even at dawn had always seemed scattered, some of it near, some far away.'

David saw Phoebe Kirkwood for the last time in December 1944. David had joined the BBC the previous year and Phoebe found a social circle in Dublin and became known for her painting. But the flame of that Woodbrook passion hadn't gone out that winter. Just before Christmas he travelled to Sutton House, where the Kirkwoods were staying. He and Phoebe spent time together walking on nearby Howth Head. He describes 'her face so quick to change, so beautifully mobile, as it had always been'.

Then comes Thomson's account of the pivotal moment of their relationship; a tender, affectionate goodbye as the tram approached to take him back to London, but which turned into something they each might have wanted to happen, for many years. The tram is cast as a metaphorical – and real – 'third party' in the scene:

> I kissed her cheek, then heard the tram again. She put her hands quickly and gently over my ears and turned me towards her lips. She kissed me passionately and for a second I was startled and did not respond. Then we kissed. Her hands were away from my ears, clasping me to her as I clasped her to me, and I did not hear the tram till the driver put its brakes on and it screamed on a strident note descending to groan towards its stopping place opposite the house. I ran to it.

Martina understands that as far as Phoebe was concerned, the relationship was on again. David was the person who didn't want to 'go back', as he put it. Either way, they never meet again. What happened next gives enduring power to the love story.

A cough he recalls hearing from her and unanswered letters are the hint. Then he ends the book starkly and without much detail.

> I remember my acute anxiety, my watching of the doormat for the post. It came at last at the end of the month on a foggy day, a single letter white on the doormat and the right shape. There were only a few words in the letter. It said what I knew it would say when I picked it up from the mat – that Phoebe was dead.

Unless the reader has a heart of stone, the David and Phoebe story is unforgettable. There would be other women in his life, one of them very significant, but Phoebe's memory had a glow that never dimmed for David Thomson.

And she was only physically gone. He had now embarked on an exciting new career, but Woodbrook – and the great love he found there – would remain.

The lily pond on the Jameson estate at Kilmacanogue, County Wicklow, in 1900. Daisy Jameson is the woman in the punt (courtesy Norman Colin).

3. A BBC Producer

The Second World War was raging on the Eastern Front when David made the journey from the family home in Pattison Road, Hampstead, to Langham Place one Monday morning to start his first real job, in the powerful BBC. He was a history graduate, had written a little, had some experience as a private tutor, but his main work experience, as he must have reminded himself that day, was as a pig rearer, a mixed-tillage farmer – along with a developed skill in horse husbandry. But all that was about to change.

David was twenty-nine when he was invited to join the illustrious Features unit of BBC Radio. The man who recruited him, Laurence Gilliam, described him several years later as 'a specialist in the art of retaining the flavour of local idiom and dialect' and a maker of 'highly original programmes'.

The setting for one of these programmes, 'Black House into White', is the Outer Hebrides. A crofter, Big Neil, is building a new house. His neighbour Ronald offers to help with the roof by gathering timber from the shore, noticing that Big Neil already had four walls built. But Big Neil is looking grave. Ronald tries to 'raise the black dog from his shoulders'.

'Thank you, Ronald. I am very thankful to you, but there will be no roof put on that house.'

'What's that you say?'

'Listen to me.' He spoke quickly now. 'When I was working there yesterday standing up on the end wall, I looked down into the lower end of the house, and I saw two coffins standing there on the floor, one on top of the other.'

David began his twenty-six-year career in BBC in 1943. He had an Oxford degree, but his rural experience on the Plains of Boyle would have given him a useful earthiness as a programme maker. The people of South Uist who feature in 'Black House into White' possessed, like the people of the west of Ireland whose heritage Thomson came to appreciate, a rich oral literature, passed on from generation to generation for hundreds of years but only remembered by some elderly people, such as Big Neil.

'But are you sure of what you saw?'

'I am and I want no illness or deaths on my family, Ronald, and I'll not bring them on to that croft.'

It was Thomson's belief, encouraged by Gilliam's leadership, that it should be preserved in some new form, perhaps best through the oral literature of radio, because the printed word, the learning of how to read and write, had eroded the memory of story-tellers.

The title of the programme comes from his discovery that many of the people he met preferred their 'black house' – a single room shared by the family and their cattle, windowless, with a hole in the thatch to let the smoke out – to the so called 'white house', erected by the county council.

Tim Dee described the perhaps surprising programme-making process of that era: 'They eavesdrop on reality and then a re-forming through the production process takes place.' Dee says we would think it extraordinary now that in a programme like 'Black House into White', which though it covered new ground, didn't actually use the voices of Uist – actors spoke their words.

The art of radio feature-making was still in its golden age in the 1940s. Television had been invented, but was in its infancy. The reflective programming of radio features was really its own art form. It was essentially intellectual, gentle, imaginative and of course non-tabloid. It survives still in many public broadcasters in Europe, but as a backwater. But in the 1940s all this was innovation.

BBC Broadcasting House, Portland Place, London.

Virginia Madsen, in a study for the University of New South Wales, Sydney in 2005, summed up this era in the BBC:

> Under the leadership of Lawrence Gilliam, when Dylan Thomas and Louis MacNeice (both poets) could produce and write 'classic' features, somewhere between drama, documentary, poetry, and what the BBC also called 'panoramas' – grand, large-scale productions based on fact, but rendered dramatically and musically with what seemed like a cast of thousands … the best the BBC had to offer.*

Madsen also quotes Peter Leonhard Braun, a veteran producer of Sender Freies Berlin (SFB), describing the advent of portable recorders: 'The portable tape recorder allowed us to give up our sedentary existence and become nomads and hunters once more. What liberation!'†

---

* Virginia Madsen: *Radio and the Documentary Imagination, The Radio Journal*, 2005.

† *Ibid.*

The man at the centre of BBC's Features unit, Laurence Duval Gilliam (1907–64), had joined the drama department in 1933. He was later made responsible for features, where he was allowed to build a creative department, largely with writers and poets. Gilliam believed: 'Broadcasting offers to the writer of our time a form of expression, and a method of publication that demands discipline, flair in the use of language to be spoken and the ability to hold the attention of a vast miscellaneous audience.'* He once described his department as an 'organized jungle'.

David had been at King Alfred School with Gilliam's Danish wife, Marianne Helweg. Gilliam decided to bring David into his team such, it seems, was his recruitment discretion. Wynford Vaughan Thomas, in describing Gilliam's power in the BBC to the authors of a book about this period, John Snagge and Michael Barsley, described him as an enormous Falstaffian figure: 'You'd go into his office and he'd say, "We're going to send you to Borneo, my dear boy. It's all right, we've got the thing fixed and you leave on such and such a plane." To enter his room often meant a passport to some marvellous liberating adventure.'†

In the Features office, intellect was all around. Another writer who came to the corridors of the BBC was surrealist poet, Philip O'Connor (1916–98). His family were Irish and Burmese and he was born in Bedfordshire and raised for a time in France. He was one of a group called the 'Wheatsheaf Writers' (they took their name from a pub of the same name). He married six times and fathered at least eight children. Thomson was very drawn to O'Connor, and, after their BBC years, corresponded with him for the rest of his life.

A towering presence in the Features Department was the Irish poet Louis MacNeice, who worked there between 1941 and 1961. MacNeice was born in Belfast in 1907 and grew up in Carrickfergus, the son of an Anglican minister later ordained bishop. MacNeice's parents were from the west of Ireland. MacNeice became a friend of the poet Stephen Spender while at Oxford and they jointly edited *Oxford Poetry* in 1929. He had been an associate of W.H. Auden and, as a left-leaning young man, a friend of the spy, Anthony Blunt. He was already well regarded as a poet when he was recruited to the BBC.

According to Laurence Gilliam, MacNeice 'won an outstanding place among modern writers by his masterly and imaginative command of the microphone'.

* Laurence Gilliam, *Features*. BBC, 1950.

† John Snagge and Michael Barsley, *Those Vintage Years of Radio* (Pitman, 1972).

This is how he began his programme 'India at First Sight':

> India is the most *foreign* country I have ever visited. If we use the word 'foreign' for Italy or Iceland, we should really find some other word for India. My first visit to India lasted from August to November 1947, when the BBC sent out a whole team of correspondents, writers and engineers to be at the birth of the two new dominions. So I got my first sight of an extraordinary country at an extraordinary time.*

He and David Thomson shared political views, a fondness for the company and inspiration that drinking brings, and of course an interest in Ireland. Martina Thomson remembered one peculiar characteristic of MacNeice – that he always leaned back, away from the person he was talking to.

MacNeice was also friendly with and shared heavy drinking sessions with the poet, Dylan Thomas, who contributed to many BBC programmes during the 1940s, though he and David Thomson don't appear to have crossed each other's path much. At one stage Thomas lived in Delancey Street, very close to Regent's Park Terrace, where David later lived, and just down the street from a great Thomson haunt, The Edinburgh Castle.

In a production of *Paradise Lost* for the Third Programme in 1947, Thomas was cast as Satan, which caused the reviewer in *The Listener*, Martin Armstrong, to write that this casting, 'swamped Milton, it swamped *Paradise Lost*, it occasionally swamped even the sense, for the louder Dylan Thomas shouts, the more his articulation deteriorates'.

In the 1940s the role of producer was only being defined and strong individuals interpreted the job as they preferred – men such as Gilliam, MacNeice, Bertie Rodgers and David Thomson. Tim Dee has an interest in this particular group. He says that while actuality is everything in modern broadcasting, in their time there was a particular literary, in their case, creative input by the producer, where they chose to embellish what they had gathered from real people. They were often called writer/producers. Dee explains it: 'You get more of a sense of they, the producers', historical and intellectual interest in the subject. The modern programme maker lets the "people speak for themselves".' There must have been a tension for people like David Thomson, he thinks; the BBC view was that the people who contributed to programmes had to have their 'hand held' by

* Gilliam, *Features*, BBC, 1950.

the institution, whereas Thomson wanted to allow freer rein to the contributor. He wouldn't have been happy with the more patronizing approach that the BBC was accused of – 'interpreting the country back to itself', as Dee calls it.

W.R. or 'Bertie' Rodgers was another of Gilliam's team who David Thomson became close to. He was born in Belfast in 1909 and part of a generation of Northern Ireland writers that included John Hewitt, MacNeice, Roy McFadden, Sam Hanna Bell and Michael MacLaverty. Rodgers was best known as a poet, though he was also a literary figure in the wider sense, being an essayist, a book reviewer, a radio broadcaster and scriptwriter, and, later in his life, a teacher. Rodgers was a Presbyterian minister at Loughgall, County Armagh in 1946, when he left to take up a job as a BBC producer. His friend Louis MacNeice, then already part of the set-up under Gilliam, largely instigated his move.

In 1949 Rodgers made 'W.B. Yeats – a Dublin Portrait', regarded as a landmark in radio feature programmes. It seems routine now as a programme-maker's approach, but it was entirely new then to use recording equipment to capture the flavour of a great personality through, as Rodgers believed, 'the memories, anecdotes and gossip of friends, critics and acquaintances'. As he said: 'The minnow of gossip can penetrate corners of history and nooks of character that the whale of erudition cannot reach.'

The contributors to the programme reflected Ireland's literary and artistic world in the mid-twentieth century: Frank O'Connor, Brinsley McNamara, Lennox Robinson, Austin Clarke, Seán Ó Faoláin, all interjecting in the discussion about the great poet. Frank O'Connor said: 'You must remember that when *I* met Yeats first he was an old and very authoritative figure, an Olympian figure. He was tall, very, very dignified, all his gestures were sweeping, his voice had a soft oratorical cadence which comes back into my ears even at this moment.'

R.M. Smyllie, who worked at *The Irish Times* and later became its editor, recalled the famous anecdote about Yeats and the circumstances of his becoming Ireland's first Nobel Laureate in 1923. A message had arrived to the newspaper that the poet had won the prize. Smyllie decided he'd ring the recipient in the hope that he's be the one breaking the news to him. Yeats hadn't heard, Smyllie recalled in the programme: 'I said "You've been awarded the Nobel Prize, a great honour for you and for Ireland," and to my amazement the first question, the only question he asked was, "How much, Smyllie, how much is it?" '

In 1950 David travelled to Ireland to make 'Songs of the Sea', fulfilling his curiosity about seals and their legends. That interest brought about his highly regarded book some years later, *The People of the Sea* (1954). 'Songs of the Sea' was broadcast in November 1950 and included music on the uilleann pipes by Séamus Ennis. One of the actors involved was Eamon Kelly, famous later for one-man shows such as 'In My Father's Time,' 'Bless Me Father' and 'Rub of a Relic'. Their relationship continued right into the 1980s when David was asked by the Peacock Theatre in Dublin to write the programme notes for Kelly's one-man show, *Roguery*. David began with the proverb, 'When a rogue kisses you, count your teeth.' Then he mentions Puck from *A Midsummer Night's Dream*, Odysseus and Tom Thumb. But the prototype of all rogues was Mercury. 'Why do we like rogues?' he wonders. 'Because of their power to survive, the way they extricate themselves from threatening situations that normal mortals would not survive. Resilience of spirit conquering brute force,' he concludes.

Eamon Kelly had made David and a group of colleagues laugh a lot when they met about thirty years previously in the County Kerry writer, Bryan Mac Mahon's bookshop in Listowel. David had decided then that he wanted him for the seals programme. 'Eamon told the seal stories beautifully. But this is over thirty years ago. Mercury has taught him a trick or two since then.'

David also met and had a close friendship with a BBC contributor, George Ewart Evans (1909–88), a pioneering oral historian. Ewart Evans published a series of books examining the disappearing customs and way of life of rural Suffolk, one title being *Ask the Fellows Who Cut the Hay*. He also wrote short stories, novels and poems. He was born and raised in the mining community of Abercynon, South Wales. In 1948 he settled with his family in Blaxhall, Suffolk, and through conversing with his neighbours he developed an interest in their dialect and the aspects of rural life, which they described. Many were agricultural labourers, born before the turn of the century, who had worked on farms before the arrival of mechanization. With the assistance of a tape recorder he collected oral evidence of the dialect, rural customs, traditions and folklore throughout East Anglia, and this work, reinforced by documental research, provided the background for his famous East Anglia books. He and David co-wrote *The Leaping Hare* in 1972.

Yet another colourful talent in Features was the poet, Terence Tiller, whose obituary Thomson would write many years later. While on assignment in Cairo during the Second World War, he wrote a series of erotic poems that were explicit for their time. 'Egyptian Dancer', was one:

The dance begins; she ripples like a curtain;
her arms are snakes
– she is all serpent, she coils on her own loins
and shakes the bells; her very breasts are alive
and writhing, and around the emphatic sex
her thighs are gimlets of oil.

But perhaps the most colourful character in the BBC was surely Francis Edward Juan Dillon, known as Jack Dillon. Also of Irish background, he was born in Manchester in 1899. He had been a member of the British army during the First World War and did service in Ireland with the Auxiliaries, the Black and Tans. He joined Features in 1941. During that same year in one of his first assignments, he and Louis MacNeice took what became an infamous recording trip on board the destroyer HMS *Chelsea*. They spent nine days patrolling the North Atlantic and indulging in late-night drinking sessions that kept the crew awake. The programme, with a its exultant title 'Freedom's Ferry', was the start of a lifetime friendship between the two men. In 1942 Dillon initiated the series, 'Country Magazine', which ran for twelve years. The Ministry of Agriculture felt such a programme would be helpful in wartime when travel between town and country was restricted. Martina Thomson remembered Jack Dillon once sleeping under the piano at a party in their house. She also recalled acting in one of his live radio programmes. When Dillon realized they risked overrunning, he crept around the actors with a large scissors, literally cutting out chunks from their scripts as they delivered them.

In 1944 David Thomson was assigned to 'Country Magazine' and worked on it for many years, becoming editor of the series in 1948. The programme, with Dillon and Thomson at the helm, is described in *Those Vintage Years of Radio* as a 'unique rural ride that has never been surpassed'. The authors* in 1972 recorded that the two BBC men were still remembered in many villages around Britain for their personalities and their largesse – at the Corporation's expense. They were something of a double act; Dillon, apparently, 'an Irish version of Groucho Marx', Thomson 'as pale and studious as a clerk in holy orders'.

* Snagge and Barsley.

In December 1949 David brought the BBC Mobile Recording Unit to the Aran Islands for an edition of the programme broadcast on the Home Service a month later, in January 1950. He enlisted Robert Flaherty, then well known as the director of *Man of Aran, Louisiana Story* and *Nanook of the North*, as the main contributor. Flaherty's script opened:

> As you know the name of the signature tune of this series is 'The Painful Plough 'and first of all I'd like to explain that this is a very unusual Country Magazine. It should have a signature tune called 'the Spiteful Spade!' On the Aran Islands there are no ploughs, no cars, no tractors, no field tools of any sort except the spade and the fork and because it is so far away we have not been able to gather all our speakers together. Their voices are all on records that we made on the islands and I shall introduce each of them as they come.

David had moved out of the family home in Pattison Road, Hampstead, and was living in rooms near Broadcasting House in Portland Place. However, a letter from his mother in November 1949 shows a certain level of care towards their thirty-five-year-old son. She writes about the new glasses they were getting for him and wishes him well on his trip to Aran.

Philip Donnellan (1924–99) was another person with Irish roots, who worked in radio before going on to become a distinguished television documentary maker, with radical and artistically subversive inclinations. Among his work were adaptations of the famous Ewan McColl and Peggy Seeger *Radio Ballads*. He later wrote a dramatized version of *Woodbrook* for radio, transmitted in 1983. He enlisted Séamus Ennis to help him find subjects for *The Irishmen*, a documentary about men who built the London Underground, immigrants known as the 'Tunnel Tigers', and other Irish labourers.

Donnellan had met Ennis after the uilleann piper and folk collector was recruited by the BBC in 1951, and described him as 'one star in a constellation of Irish talent that focussed on Features'. He describes a stellar scene one day in the Gluepot pub, close to Broadcasting House. In the bar were Ennis, Brian George, a producer originally from Donegal who with Ennis recorded material for the first-ever long-playing record of Irish traditional music, Louis MacNeice, Dylan Thomas and David Thomson, 'in his thick glasses putting down the Bass'.

> After that there were lots more times when amidst the beery uproar Séamus would suddenly murmur 'Ach … now that puts me in mind …', push his

> faded trilby back on his head, reach into an inside pocket for a fistful of whistles and choosing one, silence the bar with an instant rattling jig or delicately command consent with an exquisite slow air in which the notes would seem to hang upon the smoke.*

In 1951 David enlisted Séamus Delargy of the Irish Folklore Commission to present the introductory programme in the series 'The Irish Storyteller'. It was the start of a long collaboration. Delargy, or Séamus Ó Duilearga, founded the Irish Folklore Commission and was its director for many years. Micheál Briody says in his history of the organization, 'without him there would have been no Commission. He may have been less talented than some of his colleagues, but he was driven by a determination of steel that none of them possessed.'†

Delargy was a hard taskmaster, Briody also notes, and had a sometimes-strained relationship over the years with colleagues. He also suffered mental illness throughout his life. When it came to matters of folklore and tradition, however, he was a pivotal figure, with consummate knowledge and understanding.

Delargy and Thomson's script for the programme began:

> The folk tale was the literature of escape for countless millions of the forgotten peoples of the past, from Ireland to India, who listened to tales of wonder and of magic where all one's dreams came true, and where to all endeavours there is a happy ending; where the hero is a poor man's son, and the heroine the beauty of the world, daughter of the king of the land that never was.

In introducing programme two, which was the 'The Golden Bird of Phoenix and the Land of Youth', narrated by Paddy Sherlock. Delargy, perhaps prompted by his producer, tries to lighten up and avoid the inclination towards academic analysis of story origins, concluding with a common touch:

> Too many silly things have been written in the past by enthusiastic and ill-informed people – and as we say in Irish – *Is binn béal ina thost*: Melodious is the silent mouth.

---

* Philip Donnellan, *We Were the BBC*, 1988 (www.philipdonnellan.co.uk).

† Micheál Briody, *The Irish Folklore Commission 1935–1970* (Studio Fennica, Helsinki, 2007).

Over the years, David proved he was, intellectually and as an exponent of the radio medium, well up to the standard of his illustrious colleagues. These – and they were almost exclusively male – drank in a pub called The Stag when Features had its office in Cavendish Street; then when they were moved to the main BBC building in Portland Place, their main haunt was The George, or the BBC Club nearby. David Gentleman, an illustrator and painter whose work includes a mural at King's Cross station and who was a next-door neighbour of the Thomsons in Regent's Park Terrace, remembers being invited by David to come to the BBC and see a recording of a Samuel Beckett play, where Beckett's cousin, John, was playing the piano to accompany a children's choir. They broke for lunch and headed not to the canteen but to The George. His memory was that the play 'ripped along better' when they returned. 'I'm not a great drinker myself and I'm suspicious of people who get drunk. But I can see why David had this method. He didn't lose control, but the result was better.' He remembers on another occasion when a doctor told David that he'd have to deal with his drink problem. David apparently replied, 'It's not a problem, it's a blessing.'

The George, on Mortimer Street, one of the Features Department's haunts.

And David was writing, too. He began a novel in 1945, which was never finished and remained untitled. In Chapter 1, only handwritten in a notebook, he sets the scene, familiar for him, the house of a gentry family, the Lisburn's, called Wasselage Chase, one summer evening. It begins with an unidentified voice giving advice. The words set a gloomy scene:

> What you know to be beautiful, they will discard as pretty, something to be laughed at and put away in dark corners, derisively, where it cannot be seen. 'Pretty – pretty', they will call it, 'like a chocolate box cover.'
>
> 'Come along down with us into the sewer', they will say. Here we meet 'broken' people of various kinds.

But there's a twist. This was a just a morbid diary, thankfully for the reader: 'Dear me,' said Mrs Lisburn out loud. 'What very, very odd things your great grandfather wrote.' On one level, it's a surreal *Woodbrook:* Big House, sherry and talk of outdoor pursuits. The father is called Charlie, as in the later work. The incomplete manuscript, now in Thomson's papers, runs to several thousand words. Yet it hasn't the undisguised autobiographical form David's three published novels later took.

He also pitched articles to magazines. In 1948 he wrote a letter to Reginald Arkell, editor of *Men Only*. Not to be confused with the modern soft porn publication of the same title, it was one of the earliest men's lifestyle magazines in Britain to deliberately and self-consciously address men as consumers. The folksy subjects David tried to interest the editor in didn't grab his attention however: bird traps and their use; eel fishermen on Lough Neagh; the professional jealousy between vets and men who 'have the cure'. Another of Thomson's ideas that showed a caring for the natural world was an article on chimney sweeping where he emphatically condemned the practice of using live geese.

David had become a successful radio producer despite the impediment of mental-health difficulties that had been with him since childhood. His diary of 9 October 1945, describes returning to the BBC after one bout. Jack Dillon and Louis MacNeice were pleased to see him, he says, but apart from them he'd like to see 'every pub crawler of those regions' bombed out of existence – and their pubs, The Stag and The George. 'In the pubs were all the same faces, in the same jobs, saying the same things', he complained.

He read *Ulysses* that year, according to the diary, and agreed with Jack Dillon that the work has a 'sustained tragedy throughout': 'What deep complex characterisation, miraculous writing of dialogue, conveyance of mood – what incredible skill in setting the characters of Stephen and Bloom against each other? But the thing is past my ability to analyse – as much past it as Hamlet or Lear.'

In the diary he discussed aspects of the English language and grammar, such as cacophony and the split infinitive, addressing himself: 'You could say, "calm detachment", but try "tranquil detachment" and see what I mean. Get tranquil in some context or alone and it's a beautiful word.'

What can't be forgotten is that when David Thomson joined the BBC in 1943, Britain was at war. Winston Churchill's government, which came to power in 1940, hadn't insisted that the organization became a blunt propaganda instrument and the BBC maintained a certain autonomy. This has been credited to his Minister of Information from 1941 to 1945, Brendan Bracken, originally from County Tipperary, who famously inveigled himself into the upper reaches of the British Conservative establishment. Despite Bracken's insistence on an independent BBC, there was nevertheless patriotic duty involved for the broadcaster. At Laurence Gilliam's funeral in December 1964, the playwright Robert Kemp remembered those years with military imagery: 'He was able to recruit his men, to shape them into a force, to direct their energies. He fought their battles when the battle call was sounded and they could do no wrong in his eyes.'

Kemp also recalled an incident from sometime close to the outbreak of war in 1939. While he was walking past Broadcasting House with Gilliam, he could hear from the open window of a studio, where a programme was being prepared, Hitler's voice 'rising to a maniac's shriek' as it was being edited. 'The thought of the ordeal to come made us both sick at heart.'

Features had nerve too. The BBC archives of the period have an interesting correspondence on the broadcaster–government relationship at a time Gilliam was planning a 'Russia Night' for The Home Service. The idea was to mark the Soviet Union becoming part of the Western Allies in 1943. The Foreign Office insisted on being made aware of the planned 'theme night'. The Deputy Foreign Adviser, as he was called, a H.M. Cummings, queried the planned contribution of Louis MacNeice, after remarks made by the poet at a meeting. The Ministry also didn't want the songs they were to use in the broadcast translated to English as they might have propaganda value. Care must be taken not to 'glorify the regime' and in the 'treatment of the subject extravagance will be avoided'.

Gilliam says in a memo that the first motif of 'In Honour of Russia' was to acknowledge the part played by the Soviet armed forces, but the 'deeper purpose' is a realistic presentation of what the Russian people represent in the hope of giving listeners a wider understanding of Russian history and culture. There is little mention of the USSR or Soviet, however. The three-hour special was broadcast on 8 November 1943.

As David Thomson established himself in this company as a radio producer and writer during the 1940s, his emotional life was about to become turbulent, not for the first or last time.

4. The Kiernan Sisters

March 18th, 1946
The first beautiful and moving thing in her, that tears me with emotion as soon as she is with me after a long absence, or even after I have waited a short time in expectation, is the quality of her voice, so rare and lovely that I think it cannot be described. It is low pitched, but so are the sisters' voices; her consonants, vowels and inflexions are Irish – so are the sisters'; but in hers there's a range of feeling and expression, a pure quality.

David Thomson is writing in a notebook about one of three Dublin-born sisters, the Kiernans. He had met them through his colleague, Eric Ewens. Ewens was born in Ireland in 1917, the son of a Methodist minister. When asked where he was from in Ireland, he apparently always replied 'from all over'. He studied English at Trinity College Dublin, and went on to take a PhD. There he became friendly with another post-graduate student, the writer, politician and diplomat, Conor Cruise O'Brien. Ewens also knew Samuel Beckett and was one of the first to read *Waiting for Godot* when it was sent up to the BBC Drama Department years later. Anyone familiar with the history of Dublin and the part played by Dean Jonathan Swift will appreciate the first verses of this poem by Ewens:

A Fragment from Kubla Khant

Fag-ended pavements pave the ways
To water-music where men meet
Festooned upon the Great Dean's gaze
Prim sentinel of Werburgh Street.

Returned from Connaught or from Hell
The thirsty filter into view
Each madcap fits the bagatelle,
Fit framing for the bird's-eye view

When David became friendly with Ewens, he discovered his colleague had an Irish-born wife, Rosaleen. The couple had met during Eric's time at Trinity. David 'shared Eric and Rosaleen's life', according to Martina Thomson's account. 'David had always to rescue them, as far as I understand, financially and also taking Eric's place as a part time lecturer when Eric couldn't face it. David was very fond of Rosaleen apparently, then met Rita and so loved both of them in some way.'

Rosaleen had two sisters in London, Bernadette and Rita. They had been born in the centre of Dublin, into a family of fourteen, eleven children surviving infancy, in Patrick's Street (the area coincidentally where Ewens' poem is set, in the shadow of the cathedral). Their father owned a public house that stood on the corner with Kevin Street and his brothers farmed the family's land at Coolamber, County Westmeath. Rita, Rosaleen and Bernadette took the boat to London, where with their charm, by all accounts exceedingly good looks, and outgoing manner, were welcomed by members of the literary and artistic community.

When Ewens introduced David Thomson to the Kiernans, he was instantly attracted, first to Rosaleen, then Rita. The problem was that she was married, but their relationship began nevertheless. His letters to her are long, passionate and numerous. They show again his intense romantic side, making it easy to see how the feelings he had for Phoebe Kirkwood of *Woodbrook* haunted him for so much of his life. This is an extract from a letter to Rita, dated 30 April 1947: 'For a long time, over a week I think, I read your two letters and your postcard every night and I have had your picture on a chair by my bed all night, with a candle by it, every night, to look at.'

Rita Kiernan, with her sons, Seán and Desmond, mid 1950s (courtesy Seán Biddulph).

Later in the letter he says he feels unsure about keeping up a so sentimental a ritual. 'I can remember all our hot pleasure and the great peace and love we had afterwards, lying closely half asleep and it is sweet to think of and always will be.'

Rita Kiernan's husband, Rollo Biddulph, came from a long line of soldiers and diplomats, and at one stage the family had an estate in County Wicklow. His grandfather had been Governor of Cyprus. Biddulph was a language specialist and worked in Churchill's office, then in the secret code-breaking centre, Bletchley Park, during the war. But Rollo had a rebellious side, according to his son Desmond, and fell out with some members of his family who considered he had 'sold out' by marrying an Irish Catholic. He and Rita had two sons, Desmond and Seán and a daughter, Áine. Desmond, a psychiatric doctor who practices in London, was a young boy when David Thomson was his mother's lover and remembers him from that time. Yet his mother never revealed to him that her friendship with David was an intimate one.

His mother was 'quite a character', fond of artists and unconventional as a parent. He remembers her once bringing him to a pub as a teenager where a man made a pass at him. He remembers his mother's unshocked reaction when he told her about it: 'You've got to get used to that sort of thing.' He also recalls his mother saying years later how she found the bombing of London, curiously thrilling for her.

In the turmoil of wartime, Rita, married with children to deal with, was managing a passionate affair with a man who worked with her brother-in-law. In an undated letter from that time, David discusses the infidelity and refers to Rollo: 'But I somehow feel sure that you can't be happy with him darling, that God knows you tried very hard when he was home last time.'

Rollo was not monogamous, either. David refers to his rival's recent affair and tries, as countless lovers have done, to use it to plead with Rita: 'But one must be careful not to allow the pride and jealousy make one hold on to something one doesn't really want. My darling, I think the shock of this (the affair) makes you forget how unhappy you can be when Rollo is with you.' He seems to accept that she is trying to get back to a relationship with Rollo, admonishes himself for 'taking advantage' of someone's wartime absence. In his diary of Christmas Day 1945, a forlorn Thomson details furtive recent meetings in tea rooms and missing each other in railway stations, writing: 'When I saw her last Friday she was very beautiful, and felt happy, all her features clear and defined and the character of her face so moving that at times I could hardly speak I felt it so much.'

Discussing the rights and wrongs of their situation, he makes a physical observation – of himself: 'I am, by the way, proud of my genitals, which are good ones.' It was Rita who offered him advice when he became ill during 1946 and was evidently so gloomy that he found it hard to face work: 'You're seeing it like an outsider,' she said, according to his diary. 'But in a week or two when you've gone back you'll be part of it again and think it quite good.'

David's March 1946 notebook contains many rapturous descriptions of Rita, and of an attempt at physical passion in a phone box as they tried to find coins, she wanting a 'quick bender', he saying there was too much light from a street lamp. Then there's a reference to the natural world that often surfaces in Thomson's writing:

> When something catches her attention there is a lovely stillness of her face, alert and live. I have never seen that before in a woman or a man. I have seen

> that same motionless alert expression in young horses often, but in no other human being except her, and to find this beauty in a woman – there lies part of the joy and wonder that possesses me. I have thought many times that she has every good, pure quality of an animal.

Rita moved back to Dublin during 1946 when her mother was ill, and the correspondence continued. She lived on Ballymun Road and on South Circular Road. Towards the end of the relationship, David describes the desolation he felt when he waited and waited one day for the phone to ring: 'I am reduced to whining to myself about what I have lost; instead of being thankful for what happiness we had ...'.

Rita decided to join her husband in Vienna in 1948, but the relationship ultimately failed. She wrote many letters to David from Austria, referring in one of them to 'the mess they were all in'. Rollo's girlfriend, Lene, had a baby by this stage. The situation remained unresolved and her long letters show misgivings, agony and unhappiness. By the time Rita came back to England in 1952, David had met Martina.

In 1960, Rita began a relationship with the actor Denys Hawthorne, well-known as a performer of the work of Yeats and Beckett, and later of his fellow Ulsterman, Frank McGuinness. He and Rita married in 1970 and lived in Brighton. Hawthorne died in October 2009. Rita died barely a month later, in her ninetieth year. Her sister Rosaleen died in a home in Farnham, Surrey, in January 2014 and Bernadette has lived in Vancouver for many years. Róisin Hogan, a niece of Rita's who lives in Dublin, remembers her as larger than life even in her advanced years and always at the centre of what was going on in the extended family.

Seán Biddulph, like his brother Desmond, is fascinated by their family history and the Thomson connection. Neither is judgmental about their mother's emotional entanglements. Desmond believes that war had a very destructive effect on peoples' lives. Their mother always encouraged them to read David's books, yet never admitted to the affair. But her sons had always suspected he was once more than just a friend.

While a medical student in Dublin in 1968, Seán recalls meeting David who was in Ireland researching *Woodbrook*. The older man made an amorous suggestion to Biddulph's girlfriend at the time, later his wife. What surprised Seán was that the comment came from a seemingly reserved, intellectual-looking man. 'His bald head made him look very geeky,' Seán says. 'But when I met him by surprise once in Greece I thought differently.' Seán was staying with friends in Paros and was in a grocery store in the main town. This was during one of Thomson's sabbaticals from the BBC. 'I was standing behind someone and I suddenly realized it was David. He was getting his shopping and at the same time taking a sip of Ouzo. He invited us for dinner and a few days later we swam on the beach. David to my surprise was like a greyhound. His body was very well muscled and athletic, when one would have least expected it to be the case.'

David Thomson had mixed with the famous, travelled widely and made several lasting friendships during his early years in the BBC. But there was one person who would really stand out and influence everything he did thereafter, following their chance meeting in 1952.

5. Martina

'He had something I call melting. He melted towards you … towards me – and of course towards other women. He didn't protect himself, as others do.'

One day early in 1952, Martina Schulhof, a twenty-seven-year-old Berlin-born actress, came to BBC Broadcasting House to meet a radio producer, Dorothy Baker. While she was there, Baker suggested she should also meet another producer – his name was David Thomson. According to Martina, when she went into his office, David stepped backwards, fell over his chair and landed on the floor. Whether it was his short sightedness that caused the accident, or the shock of Martina's glamour, the attraction was instant. Martina for her part recalled modestly: 'I think I made a big impression on him.'

Enter the most important woman in David Thomson's life. For their first date, David went to see Martina in a play in a small theatre in Notting Hill. She remembers he bought her what appeared to be the entire stock of daffodils from a nearby stallholder.

'Mind that man,' Martina's mother said. 'I think he's a little drunk.'

'But I didn't mind him – in that sense.' Martina recalled. 'In fact, I went home with him that night.'

A publicity photo of Martina Thomson, early 1950s (courtesy Luke Dodd).

The egalitarian in David liked the idea that Martina had once worked in a factory, and yet her theatrical and seemingly exotic family background also appealed to him. Her mother, Magdalena Maria (Lene) Hoellering was born in Vienna in 1899. Martina's uncle, her mother's brother, was George Hoellering Jnr, a theatre and film producer who had worked with Bertholt Brecht. He later directed the film version of T.S. Eliot's *Murder in the Cathedral* in 1951, in which Martina, who used the stage name Martina Mayne, had a small part in the chorus.

Her mother had married Erich Schulhof in 1922. He was co-owner of the family business, which made hat feathers. The couple and their two children, Thomas (born in 1923) and Martina (born in March 1925), lived in a large villa with domestic servants in Berlin–Wannsee. In 1938 Erich Schulhof was forced to sell his business due to the Aryanization policy in Nazi Germany. He didn't receive any money from the sales of either the business or the family home. In remembering, Martina casts Germany in a negative light: 'I think I took a certain amount of comfort from the fact I was Austrian, not German,' recalled Martina. 'But I didn't realise that the Austrians made excellent Nazis.'

Martina remembered a grim Berlin. 'As a child I was frightened by the uniforms and the awful clicking of the boots. Artists kept disappearing and one, a friend of the family, shot himself.'

Martina wrote a poem after Kristallnacht (9-10 November 1938), the night that Jewish businesses all over Germany were attacked and destroyed.

This extract from the poem, 'Sad Streets', recalls black boots on cobbles, a burgled shop and a burning synagogue.

The milk-cart rattles over cobblestones,
the high, clear sound of Huebner's bell,
froth to the brim in the jug they hold,
rides can be cadged, the pony stroked.

Then milk-vans come on rubber tyres,
'hurry up, quick,' a hooter calling,
blunt bottles handed over coldly –
still it is summer and she loves her frocks.

But listen, black boots now click in the street,
a staccato flagsong disrupts the day.
The dog is poisoned, lies yelping and dies
while their father keeps vigil stretched on the sofa.

From her desk at school she sees a man fall
across the window: a pause in the classroom.
'A shop's been burgled, the church is on fire!'
'Ah, you don't know', says the piano teacher.

While still at school, Martina had a romantic attachment to a local boy she referred to as R. His parents were members of the Nazi Party, and he himself joined the army and served on the Russian front. She describes him as a sort of leader of the class, clever and good-looking, also a talented pianist. Martina thought that R's parents joined the Nazis out of a sense that they had to share in the fate of their country.

After the war, Martina got in touch with R's parents and learned that they'd lost him and their other son. His fellow soldiers throughout the war had shielded R apparently because of his gifts as a pianist. However, as the German army retreated, he left his encampment on one occasion to search for food. He was returning with a chicken when a sniper shot him.

R's parents gave Martina a collection of letters and poems he'd written to her throughout the war years, expressing his devotion. Martina looked back on it as a 'love and death story' with similarities to David's relationship with Phoebe Kirkwood in Ireland, as it happens also in the 1930s. The fact that this boy was serving in the Nazi army's brutal campaign in Russia, while her family were victims of the regime, she stoically accepted as 'just fate'.

The Schulhofs were one of the few fortunate Jewish families. Erich Schulhof escaped to England in autumn 1938. Magdalena, with Martina and Thomas and her mother, reached London in November the same year. Erich and his brother tried to re-establish their business in England, but the factory was destroyed in bombing raids in 1940. In that year Erich Schulhof was interned as an enemy alien. In the meantime the family moved to Gloucestershire, where Magdalena spent most of the war years working on a farm. In 1942 Erich received permission to work and became a teacher. He was made redundant in 1945 when the teacher he had replaced returned from military service. He died suddenly in 1948. Magdalena later remarried and Martina attended RADA in London and became a radio and stage actress.

The Thomsons youngest son Ben recalls that his mother always wanted to deny her German background. She took elocution lessons to get rid of her accented English, and not just because she was seeking a career in acting. When Martina was asked ever where she came from, she would reply 'from everywhere.' Her brother Thomas, on the other hand, never lost his German accent. David Gentleman, a family friend for many years, only discovered the Schulhof name when he was asked to write Martina's obituary in 2013. Ben recalls being on a beach in Wales once with his mother when she overheard a German couple nearby. He was surprised by the way they annoyed her because they spoke with 'upper class Berlin accents'.

Martina soon got to know the Features Department's *modus operandi* and became involved in David's programmes on occasions. She described the loose, informal programme-making process under Gilliam: 'If David said he'd like to make a programme about the songs of the Sami people, Laurence would just say, "Ok, what do you need?" '

Martina and David sometime in the 1950s (courtesy Martina Thomson).

In 1955 he did just that and made *Songs of the Lapps*. The opening to the programme is elegant and simple.

> ANNOUNCER: This is the BBC Third Programme.
> Songs or jojks of the Lapps.
> TURI: The Lapp song is jojking. This is a way of recalling other folk: some are remembered with hate, some with love, and some with sorrow. And often these songs concern certain places, or animals … the wolf and the reindeer.

One of the participants was 'The Traveller,' David Thomson himself:

> I found that every Lapp in this part of the country had his own jojk – a jojk that characterizes him or his family so clearly that it is recognized by all who know him. The jojk of a heavy, stupid man would make people laugh. The jojk of a swift, good herdsman would start a conversation of admiring reminiscences.

Martina accompanied David on the trip to the north of Sweden, an arrangement that in today's media world would seem almost unprofessional. They stayed four weeks and lived mostly in a hut called a kota, similar to an igloo, made of bent branches covered with peat. Martina recalled in 2013 that the Lapp people didn't take too kindly to her being pregnant and unmarried.

Martina also discovered David had been engaged to a woman called Jacqueline Wynmalen in 1934, when he was only twenty. The couple had even acquired a house in Hampstead. Wedding presents were arriving. Then Jacqueline changed her mind and went back to a previous relationship. She married Richard Goodwin, an American-born economist, in 1937. Martina said: 'It was one of the few things David didn't talk about. Perhaps it was quite hurtful, though he once pointed out the house they were going to live in.'

Wynmalen's many letters to David show a restrained type of courtship, such as arrangements to meet for walks. They were both students in Oxford. There's a reference much later in his life by David to Wynmalen, in a notebook of May 1966: 'I've thought of her lately. Why? Thought of Blenheim Park, kissing her by force, and the small old house in the village where I stayed alone one night. Why did I go there? Refusing to relinquish my misery about parting with her.'

So in 1952, David began a passionate and as we will see, sometimes turbulent relationship with Martina, but which was to last for the remainder of his life. David was at this time working on *The People of the Sea*, his first book. A letter from the early weeks of their relationship from Martina to David (then working in BBC Bristol) in 13 May 1952, reveals a hint that she understood his mental complexity:

> Darling –
>
> Feeling vital and ravishing and thanking you for it . . . what lovely weeks we spent yesterday. I feel wholesome like after a long holiday. Are you as happy?

In 1954 David was on secondment from the BBC to UNESCO Radio in Avenue Kléber, Paris. In a letter to him on 23 April Martina reports that Laurence Gilliam's children were staying with her, then asks, 'Don't like you sad, you aren't now are you?' While working for UNESCO, he went to Liberia and Turkey and made programmes about both countries. Martina eventually joined David in Paris. He had found an apartment near Montparnasse goods yard. 'Paris life was utterly exciting,' Martina recalled, 'but then what do I do? I ran off with one of the artists we knew.' The new couple went to Italy, to a little village south of Naples. 'A few months later I came back – pregnant!' Martina and David resumed their relationship, despite the fact that he clearly wasn't the father of the child. This was an emotional time-bomb that would detonate years later.

To add to the complications in Paris, Martina had a rival to contend with; a ballet dancer, Nika Nilanowa. She and David met in the summer of 1954.

There are letters from their relationship right up to 1961. Nika describes her passion for David, amid details of a hectic schedule as a dancer. In one, she enthuses about a production of *The Firebird*. In August 1954, she wrote to David: 'I am reading *The People of the Sea* and dreaming about seals. I can imagine them dancing. I love your book very much. In each word I feel your heart.'

David's relationship with Nika had cooled to cordiality by December 1956, when she writes to say she was pregnant and had married a Hungarian oboe player from the orchestra in The Hague where she had been working. Then she asks David to give her best to Martina and revealingly asks: 'Did she get her daughter? I should be very proud if she could call her Nika, as she asked me in a letter long time ago.' A letter from Nika in March 1959 has no hint of any lingering love affair and she signs it, 'All the best to you.'

Nika wrote to Martina two years after David's death in 1990, addressing her as 'darling Martina': 'Thinking of David, my heart gets warm and happy. I feel so wonderful having met you and him ... this love will be always with you, dear, dear Martina.' Knowing that Martina had the evidence, as it were, she instructs 'do whatever you think with my letters'.

David with Nika Nilanowa, undated but probably mid 1950s (courtesy Martina Thomson).

During the work on *The People of the Sea*, David introduced Martina to Ireland, through his friend, Tomás de Bhaldraithe (1919–96), an Irish-language scholar who was born Thomas MacDonagh Waldron and changed his name to the Irish version. He is best known for his *English–Irish Dictionary*, published in 1959, and for the language laboratory he set up in University College Dublin, the first of its kind in any university in Ireland.

De Bhaldraithe arranged for Martina to stay with a family in Spiddal. It was the beginning of her love for the Irish countryside, people and pubs. The Thomsons later holidayed in Connemara with the de Bhaldraithe family on a number of occasions. Tomás's daughter, Clíona de Bhaldraithe-Marsh, a former academic in University College Dublin, recalls being asked as a young woman by Martina to bring David into the centre of Dublin to buy a new jacket. The shopping became a memorable pub crawl for her and there was no jacket bought.

Ben Thomson describes his father as a very thoughtful and kind man and, infidelity aside, says his father was completely devoted to his wife. He would leave notes for her in different parts of the house, sometimes mentioning the route he would take home so she could meet him, he recalls. 'They had a lovely life together. And her relationship with him with regard to his writing couldn't be replaced.' On the other hand, Ben also recalled his father being interested once in a girlfriend he had. 'I went out of the room and when I came back, she was sitting on his lap. And she fifteen!'

And what of Martina in this respect? Ben says his mother once said to him that before having children she was unfaithful, but had vowed to herself that after having her sons, she wouldn't be. On the other hand, he recalls her friendship with the writer C.L.R. James, who once lived in their basement flat and believes that she would bring one of the boys to a dinner date with James as 'cover'. David refers to this relationship in a passage in *In Camden Town*. While he isn't specific about the nature of the relationship, it did cause jealousy on his part.

Luke Dodd, who became Martina's executor, summed up her and David's relationship: 'It was never going to be simple and monogamous. They always goaded each other. I think of their relationship a little like Joyce and Nora.' Martina once told him about a time when there was a woman that David was close to and all three ended up in bed together in Regent's Park Terrace. Though he thinks sex wasn't involved, it was an attempt to 'lance the boil', as it were. Anyway, equilibrium was restored.

Melanie Cuming (née Daiken), a close friend of Martina Thomson.

Another recollection comes from Melanie Cuming (née Daiken), who was born in Dublin and first met David after he had produced a play for the BBC, *South Circular* written by her father, Leslie Daiken, a writer and prominent member of Dublin's Jewish community in the 1940s and 1950s. Daiken knew Conor Cruise O'Brien, who suggested he apply for a post in Legon University in Accra, Ghana. Melanie's mother joined him and worked as an assistant to Cruise O'Brien, when he became vice-chancellor of the University of Ghana in 1962.

Melanie and her husband Patrick had a long relationship with the Thomson family. 'She was stunningly beautiful. She was beautiful when she was in her 80s. And she was an actor, a sculptor, a poet, a painter, and an art therapist – very good at that. Amazingly talented. And she had a difficult time with David. She did tell me often that she found it very hard when he went off with these other women. He would admit it all to her afterwards, but he was a ladies' man – from the very beginning.' In trying to understand why his infidelity was tolerated over so many years, Melanie thinks that it's possible that Martina got some kind of thrill or charge out of it: 'It might have made him more exciting for her. Who knows?'

Melanie has another interesting theory about David Thomson's emotional needs: 'He needed to feel that he was able to fall in love. It wasn't necessarily that he wanted to have sex with other women, it was the act of falling in love and the high that came with it that mattered to him.'

At different stages of David's life, his 'home from home', as Martina described it, was the Halliwick Hospital in Friern Barnet, North London. Silvio Benaim was a consultant psychiatrist there and prescribed lithium for David. Martina recalled that David hated taking it, but mostly did, and it controlled his frequent highs. These she remembered as in many ways good for *him*, but disruptive for everyone else.

David found different ways of dealing with his depression. He read one particular book, the *Temple Complete Shakespeare*, over and over. Martina also remembered a time when they were at their house in Norfolk, a converted schoolhouse. She remembered David endlessly walking a pony, which had a soft-hoof condition, around the schoolyard.

Melanie Cuming taught Ben Thomson piano in the 1960s and recalls David's deep depression. 'He would sit in that room, his study, on a chair in the dark,' she recalls, 'not writing or reading. You knew David was depressed and you just had to be quiet. Martina had such vitality. Another person would have been worn down by it. David wasn't vital – he was thoughtful and reflective. She was always vigorous and joyful even when David was depressed. She was an exceptional person. She did it all – he just let things happen. And she remained serene.' By contrast, Luke Thomson says his father could be strong-willed and fearless on occasion and believes that David was really the stronger person in the relationship. Martina's long period of grief after David's death may be evidence for this view.

Ben recalls his father having less manic moods when on lithium, except when he deliberately didn't take it in order to get high. 'It worked, but he always had a struggle with it. When he had a manic mood, he could literally talk himself hoarse.' Tim Thomson recalls this aspect of David: 'He went "up" and that was interesting, then he'd go down and you didn't see that much of him, then he'd be in hospital. It happened several times.'

Once, during a high period, David became obsessed with black skin. It was the lead-up to the 'East Africa episode'. David told Martina in a coffee shop in Camden Town that he might not be able to resist this allure. With his imagination on overdrive that day, he was linking the colour of coffee beans to skin pigment. This was the beginning of the episode that later became his novel, *A Break in the Sun*.

Ben, the youngest of the Thomsons' sons, at his home in Brighton.

In the summer of that year, 1961, Laurence Gilliam sent David on an assignment to Tanganyika, as Tanzania was then. It was then one of the world's poorest countries, and David was sent to make a programme about its recently achieved independence from Britain. Julius Nyerere, its charismatic leader, was a capable orator and organizer, and his readiness to work with different interest groups was a significant factor in independence being achieved without bloodshed. It won him many friends in the West. David was personally drawn to the 'African Socialism' of Nyerere. Inspired by idealism, the new leader embarked on a collectivization of agriculture that, while a lot less brutal than that of the USSR, was in the end equally unsuccessful.

David's African excursion hit trouble early on. A combination of the climate, the exotic location and his own vulnerability contributed to a breakdown in Dar es Salaam, where he was admitted to hospital. The family was alerted. His sister Joan, always the closest of his siblings, wrote to him on 20 August: 'I hope the hospital is nice and they are looking after you well.'

Having recovered somewhat, he was travelling back to England when he stopped en route in Mombasa, Kenya. Here, female company proved irresistible.

He went to a brothel, Martina says, 'and there he met a most wonderful girl, who was half-Japanese, I think. They only had a few days together, but it was very intense.'

David met Jeni Johana in a bar in the in Tangana district of Mombasa. Her photo (she later featured in his novel, *A Break in the Sun*), and receipts from the bar, are in the Thomson papers. On 15 August, Martina wrote:

> I dreamt you loved a girl – a rejuvenated Isla Cameron [a well-known Scottish singer and actress of the time], and the room was now for her, you locked it when you went out. I wept and wept as I went about the house. The worst thing was to see you so callous and thoughtless. I saw you carrying two packets of lentils for her supper.
>
> Why don't you leave? You said, 'because of the children.' I screamed back at you. I was longing to go away.
>
> This dream has been oppressing me all day. It's you not writing I think, that has given me the feeling that you have turned away from me.

David later used some of the same phrases from this letter in his novel, *A Break in the Sun*.

During the long voyage to Europe and England, David had the presence of mind to write home to London to give a message of reassurance. In this letter to his doctor, Jerry M. Slattery, in Swiss Cottage, he writes:

> Dear Jerry,
>
> I expect you have heard from gossip in 'The George' that I got shut up in the 'looney bin' in Dar [Dar es Salaam] for a week. I am quite all right now and am travelling home by ship.

David also had a clarification. He wanted the doctor not to tell the BBC that the hospital in Dar-es-Salaam had referred to a fear of flying in their letter to Dr Slattery, as this could jeopardize David being sent on future foreign assignments: 'This would be hell for me.' David's travel expenses claim to his understanding employer in October 1961 contains some details; he explains his relapse came as the ship was approaching Marseilles and when the doctor on board, a Dr Black, hadn't the necessary drugs, he attended a Dr Abeille in the city.

After arriving in Marseilles in September he made his way to Paris. It's a measure of her organizational ability that Martina had written to him as 'Passenger on the SS *Uganda*' on 5 September, with a domestic matter: 'Now do you want to buy the schoolhouse in Edingthorpe from Mr Hale for £650? Let me know by the 20th.' The Thomsons did later buy this house in Norfolk, a disused schoolhouse, which became their country home. Another Martina letter to American Express follows on the 18th, she, aware now of another woman: 'Have just read your letters. This is torture. You don't tell me anything about your girl. Are you going off to live with her? Let me come and meet you in Paris, say the 23rd ...?'

She continues: 'I never knew you had an affair with Nika. I miss love making, you told me not. Will you see her sometime, will you dream of her? Was it the half-open door and the half-open girl? I wanted to go and find you immediately in Paris, but Timmy's birthday, how could I miss it?'

'Then a miracle happened,' Martina recalled in 2013. After she held a birthday party for her son Tim's sixth birthday, she decided to take the overnight train to Paris in the hope of meeting her errant husband. She reached Paris went to an American Express office as a starting point. A forlorn letter from her, left at American Express, dated 18 September 1961, survives:

> Darling – I do hope I'll find you it has been hard not to come, to keep on visiting and knowing you're around somewhere ill. Where can we meet?
>
> Then please ask for a message at UNESCO Radio Department.
>
> So hoping for you,
>
> M
>
> All well at home

She was in the queue at the same office another day when she noticed a man ahead of her in what looked like pyjamas. It was David in his 'oriental outfit', she recalls. So they were reunited.

When he came home, David was admitted again to the Halliwick Hospital. A letter to him from Martina while she was working in Germany shows some kind of equilibrium has been restored to their relationship. In fact she describes in the letter meeting African students in a bar one night: 'I flashed my Zanzibar jingles – with no success, all too well trained or I wasn't blonde enough. I wanted to ask them did they come from East Africa. Some looked nice. But maybe I'd have to pay for it, like you.'

A letter she wrote while on a ship to the Netherlands on 26 September that year, as she travelled to an acting engagement, is perhaps an elegant bookend to the East Africa episode.

> Lovely leaving Harwich last night silently in the moonlight. Thought of you naturally in your boat at night. So then I tried the bar and looked at the enemy. Looked too for a sea prince. A little Bernard Rebel was all there was.
>
> So then to my cabin, shared with a mother and little girl who cried out at night and I jumped up thinking 'which one is it?'

Later in the letter she wrote: 'I'm even surprised that I want to get back to our daily life. Do you, I wonder? I know we'll always have to leave room for the great, unforeseen things like East Africa for which I love you, darling, I do.' Most women wouldn't have forgiven David's behaviour, but Martina excused him on the basis of what she termed a kind of fatal attraction he had for certain types of women, and his mental health – not mentioning her own generosity.

The women, David's 'baits', as Martina referred to them, were 'preferably tall and slim, fair haired, open (not sophisticated), humorous a little, alive to encounters and maybe rather often had some sadness in their lives. When I say "open" I mean he wanted to see a little into their souls.'

The Thomsons didn't actually get married until the summer of 1964. The ceremony took place in the Town Hall, Euston Road. The witnesses were their great friend Philip O'Connor, and John Bunting who had published *The People of the Sea*. In an unconventional touch, instead of a reception they went across to St Pancras station and had drinks in the bar there, Martina recalled. 'I was presented with flowers and some sugared almonds, pink and white. It seemed all very lovely and then David and I fetched our boys from school at Gospel Oak.' Yet Ben Thomson says the boys didn't know about the wedding, having always assumed their parents were married already.

David's papers contain a letters from Phyllis Miller, with an address in Templeogue, Dublin, who apparently met David on several occasions when she visited friends in Snape, near Edingthorpe in Norfolk where the Thomson's had a house. A note on one of the letters which are among his papers, in Martina's handwriting, simply says: 'Girlfriend of David during *Woodbrook* time.'

Also among his papers there's a notebook from May 1978 in which he reflects on girls, as he calls them. Martina had told him 'once or twice' that he was 'bad about girls' – the female characters – in his novels. He mulls this over in his diary. In the writings of E.M Foster, he laments, the girls don't stir your passions. 'George Eliot stirred my passions when I was sixteen, made me fall in love with her.'

He is then reminded of flowers, as the Chelsea Flower Show has just begun. 'I love daffodils, certain roses, Sweet William and hate irises and hydrangeas. But it's not the Sweet William I write about; it's the effect of the Sweet William on my senses.'

Martina would have found the following passage reassuring:

> A first glance at a beautiful face and body is a momentary pleasure. An hour can destroy it, unless it is confirmed by talk, by soul together with body, by everything in me and her going together – at least for a few days. Sometimes, as with M [as he often referred to Martina], the going together lasts – with her it is certain by now that it will last till one of us dies. But it started with a sudden and instinctive glance.

Some of David's BBC colleagues became family friends. Their circle would be regarded now as bohemian. At one stage Philip O'Connor spontaneously took up with an American millionaire. He told her he needed £15 a week to give his wife since he'd be leaving her; he also 'needed' a two-week safari and he wanted to live in France. She agreed to all after one night, Martina says: 'Then he'd come back to visit us and say it's all over with that "terrible woman", and so on. Then he'd ask us to pay for the taxi to catch the train back to France to her. We both liked him. He was so alive. I think our three sons all wrote school essays on him!' Ben Thomson recalls: 'He was a nutcase – a brilliant nutcase. I really liked him.'

In a letter O'Connor wrote to David in October 1961 when David was a patient in the Halliwick Hospital, we get a sense of his 'larger than life' quality:

> My Dear David,
>
> At last I have the distinction of having a friend in a loony bin – I think this is the only honourable place for a person working in the BBC to be, and I feel that you are extremely brave to be the first person to take this sensible step.

Many years later, after David's death, Martina met O'Connor in France and discovered that his marriage had survived. By that stage he had written his most famous book, an autobiography, *Memoirs of a Public Baby*, detailing how his mother abandoned him and his siblings to a woman in France, then returned to look for them, causing turmoil. As another example of trauma in the Features Department, Laurence Gilliam's Danish wife, Marianne Helweg, left him and began a relationship with Bertie Rodgers, Gilliam's employee. They married in 1953.

Martina Thomson in her kitchen at 22 Regent's Park Terrace, Camden Town, in June 2013.

After David retired from the BBC in 1969, Martina taught painting to children. She went on to specialize in art therapy and its effectiveness in dealing with psychiatric problems. In 1989 she wrote *On Art and Therapy – an Exploration*. In 2013, Martina revisited her childhood when she translated a collection of poetry, *Panther and Gazelle,* by Paula Ludwig, a fellow Austrian who_regularly visited the Schulhof family home in Berlin when it was an artistic oasis during the rise of Nazism.

Martina lived in the home she and David shared in Camden Town up until her death in September 2013, aged eighty-eight. She always maintained the room she originally designated as David's writing room when they moved into the house in 1955. Martina was immensely proud of his literary legacy – created mostly within those four walls – and her part in it. David often described her as his best editor. All the books he wrote since they met in 1952 were dedicated to her, apart from the *Danny Fox* series, which were dedicated to their sons. In their elegant kitchen she summed up David, the man and husband: 'David's feelings were very near to the surface all the time. I really liked this.'

In giving all of David's papers in 2006 and 2011 to the National Library of Scotland in Edinburgh, with virtually no restrictions attached, Martina was making an important statement about their relationship. Sally Harrower, curator at the library, put it this way: 'I get the impression she had gone through everything and wanted the real David to be represented in all his complexity. Fascinating material. And it all makes Martina rather more wonderful, too – love like hers is quite something.'

The actress Jeananne Crowley came to know the Thomsons in the 1970s after she reviewed *Woodbrook* for *The Irish Times*. The book had made a huge impression on her; she was thrilled to meet its author. Many years later, she describes David as 'spiritual aristocracy'. She also reflects on the couple's relationship. 'He wasn't what they call "fit for purpose" in the modern world, hence Martina was utterly essential to him having any sort of well-being. Basically someone like David needed "minding" but of course that was not something ever said aloud.'

Several years after David's death, Martina celebrated the memory of their life and shared relationship with Ireland:

David

Your chair I can touch now, it doesn't attack me,
your coat still hangs there but has no power.
All around here what there was is expended.
You don't disturb me. Perhaps I'm forgetting you.

But there's no safety on the roads beyond Galway
where snipers linger at crossroads – signposts
with names barely familiar target my chest.
Spiddal, Oughterard, Carraroe and Carna.

Sleepwalker, I'm drawn to the pub by the pier,
the one with the fish-shed askew beside it,
and on entering know we sat here –
I take the black drink of your absence.

In 2013, twenty-five years after David's death, Martina remembered details of their domestic life: 'David was the breakfast cook, a full breakfast. Afterwards we made the bed together. He always kissed my nightie, smiling. He often groaned terribly while shaving. He said it was with shame at something he had done.'

Martina knew she had, all those years before, fallen in love with a troubled genius, an emotionally complex man. All relationships contain mystery and create speculation as to who gives or takes most, who is the stronger or the weaker. Martina's love for David was expressed in one way by the extent of her grief, acknowledged by family and friends, after his death. She recollected a detail from their life in her diary of 1988:

> The cow parsley brought a stab of memory – it was the ubiquitous flower in Norfolk, it was the summer season itself. When we bicycled down the lanes, when we picnicked, when we drank in the garden, everywhere flowering cow parsley surrounded us. Eating and working in the house it shimmered outside every window. You said you loved it and it's now for me the very distillation of our Norfolk summers. Such thoughts, I'm told, will eventually make me happy – not yet, not yet, they tear at me.

6. Challenges at the BBC

David Thomson was largely unconcerned with strategic and policy matters in the BBC, preferring to plough his own furrow as a programme maker. There is no indication in his papers that he was exercised about channels and their policies or identities, it was only output that really concerned him. Management positions didn't attract him, either. He had his own inner concept of advancement, which came from the combination of the opportunities the BBC afforded him and his own creative impulses outside the day job. It was a relatively relaxed working environment, typified by the tolerance of 'liquid lunches' – and even some employees' alcohol dependence. The media landscape was completely different from today.

Broadcasting was still a relatively new medium and there was much discussion and debate about its role. For his first three years there, BBC Radio had just two channels, the Light Programme and The Home Service. In September 1946 the radio dial got a new addition: The Third Programme. It was unashamedly highbrow. This was the thinking at the time, an attempt by the broadcaster to 'improve people' – whether they liked it or not. But broadcasting was only in its infancy and the people who ran the BBC felt that there was a higher cultural purpose to be adhered to, given the power of this relatively new medium, and it was their responsibility to deliver it. A public debate followed that revolved around 'high brow', 'low brow' and accusations of 'elitism', documented by, among others, Kate Whitehead. She quotes the *Daily Mirror*'s 'cauterisation' of both the new channel and the BBC's Director General at the time, William Haley, referring to his innovation as 'Haley's Third Symphony for orchestra and two listeners'. Lord Reith, the famous advocate of 'public service broadcasting' and BBC boss until 1938, was another dissenter from the idea, though a more considered one: 'The Third Programme, positively and negatively, is objectionable. It is a waste of precious wavelength. Much of its matter is too limited in appeal, the rest should have a wider audience.'*

Features under Laurence Gilliam, who had made programmes for the Home Service, now had a new creative outlet, giving a boost to Gilliam's vision. This is when he set about recruiting literary figures. David Thomson played his part in this creative milieu, with programmes like 'Black House into White', inspired by his travels for 'Country Magazine'.

Humphrey Carpenter, in his book, *The Envy of the World: Fifty Years of the Third Programme and Radio 3*, suggests that there was a wish by officialdom that the general population, of mixed educational level, would row in behind the ideal involved. So what was the Third schedule? He gives an example of one night (The Third was evening, only), Friday 16 April 1948, coincidentally when Thomson's 'The Great Hunger' was being broadcast. The opening programme was a play, followed by a twenty-minute piano recital of a work, not by Chopin or Beethoven, but Scriabin. Dr J Bronowski then gave the third of a series of talks, *The Common Sense of Science*; Between 7.30 and 8.40 there was a programme of Vivaldi concertos; Thomson's programme then lasted for fifty-five minutes till 9.35; a performance by the BBC Chorus of works by Bach and British composer, Edward Rubbra, was followed by the lightest item of the night, perhaps, a comic monologue by Ruth Draper, though its title was consistent with the evening: 'At an Art Exhibition'. A programme of Victorian authors' writings on the emancipation of women followed that. At 10.55 the choir of the Brompton Oratory provided the music for a script on 'Early Christian Music'. The final programme was a selection of poems by Vachel Lindsay.

* Kate Whitehead: *The Third Programme – a Literary History* (Clarendon Press, Oxford, 1989).

The programmes that night were the subjects of a Listeners Research Report. A theme that was echoed and re-echoed, Carpenter notes, among those that were questioned, was that they 'were looking for programmes that were not so far removed from their experience that they feel hostile to them' and that the Third was 'emphasising unfamiliar works at the expense of known classics'.*

Thomson's programme would surely, not just to Irish ears, have had the widest appeal of that night's programmes. This media debate continues to the present day – what is 'good' or 'bad' in programming; what is 'quality' at all?

The Third was born at an exciting time, says Carpenter. Labour had come to power with a huge majority; there was a radical programme – by today's standards at least – with nationalization of many industries. The National Health Service was inaugurated a month after the Third's first transmission on 29th September 1946.

After The Third Programme went on air, Thomson and Features still contributed to the Home Service – and it wasn't all highbrow material. In 1960 David put out word in the national press looking for lazy people. There was ample press coverage of this search, some of it a little sarcastic about the BBC. David described what he was looking for in literary terms – what he called 'Oblomovs', from a character of the Russian writer, Ivan Goncharov; a person who practises laziness and thoroughly enjoys it. There was a tremendous response, judging from the large file in his papers. A letter from a Mrs K. Mills in Summerhill, Birmingham, asked if it wasn't too late, 'It would be a blessing for me if you could make some use of my lay-about husband for your programme. He seems to get along without even getting fresh air.'

Another from a Leslie Massey in Leeds, declared: 'It is said in Women's Mirror that you want to hear from the LAZY. Well here I am. THE original, you must excuse errors, the spelling, too lazy to use a dicktionery [his spelling].' A letter from Cardiff had the admission: 'I sincerely loath work, for its own sake and because it is a waste of life, which is already too short.'

David replies to many of the letters writing that he's sorry, but 'You don't seem lazy enough for the programme I intend.' Many of the letters are really long and mostly very articulate, turning Thomson's trawl into something more fascinating altogether.

---

* Humphrey Carpenter, *The Envy of the World, Fifty years of the BBC Third Programme and Radio 3* (Weidenfeld & Nicolson Ltd, London, 1996).

A Mrs South in Cambridgeshire outlined her theory: 'The lazy person is actually an idealist. I am. Up to eight years ago I was a busy person, normal in every way, things were coming up to my ideal. Then, through no fault of my own, things crashed. Oh nothing outsiders would notice. And nothing frivolous like a broken love affair.'

'Laziness' was broadcast on the Home Service on Sunday, 23 July 1961 at 10.10 am. It opens with David himself making a clever justification for opening with a musical pun, the song 'Lazybones':

> DAVID THOMSON: Nearly thirty years ago in the summertime I used to annoy our neighbours with this song, sung out of tune by me in bed on sunny mornings with the windows open. One of them even got me out of bed by ringing up from across the road and telling me to stop.
>
> DISC: 'Lazybones'.
>
> Two years ago, with it still in my head, I went with a tape recorder to my friends in Lotus Land and asked them how they felt.

The testimonies that mentioned fear and anxiety must have reminded Thomson of his own difficulties. In another part of the programme his narration makes use of Osbert Sitwell's essay, 'In Praise of Indolence'.

> 'The idle man is usually a good natured one; at worst, harmless; whereas men who do the harm, the Napoleons and Lenins and Hitlers and rabid newspaper peers, are obliged by their natures to be ever frantically striving ... poor creatures, they cannot rest till they're worn out.'
>
> But anyway after all this I realised that none of us had dared to say what we thought idleness was. Can anyone define it?

And what of David's day-to-day working environment in Langham Place and later in Portland Place? Dorothy Baker, the colleague who had introduced him to Martina in 1952 and who had since been promoted, appears to have been quite tough as a script editor. She wrote a memo to David in July 1955 dismissing a proposal he had made to make a programme from a script by a David Shelly Nicholl, *The End of the Cruise*. 'I do not care for this specimen,' she says. 'I do not find Mr Nicholl light, I find him verbose and that is a great fault for radio.'

As might be expected, David didn't always give the corporate line when rejecting scripts, once expressing scepticism about the institutional climate: 'We are giving a wide interpretation to feature which in BBC jargon is supposed to be a factual documentary,' he wrote in 1955 to an aspiring contributor Marghanita Laski, a writer who later became a regular BBC panellist. Some proposals came from colourful characters. Ludwig Koch's letterhead stated 'MBE, author, broadcaster, lecturer and recorder of nature sounds'. He signs his letters as different historical characters, and makes very original programme pitches:

> Dear Son of Thom,
>
> Johannes Brahms has asked me to broadcast a short description of his life, which he has written down with his pen, and I have transferred it on a modern writing machine. Up to you to make alterations, as you knew Johannes much better than I did.
>
> If nothing prevents me I shall have the honour to come to you in Broadcasting House, Glasgow on Wednesday the 17th of July 1973 and I took notice that you send me a helicopter.
>
> votre ami,
>
> Louis Napoleon Bonaparte

There's an interesting insight into the BBC mindset of the time in a memo David wrote to Gilliam in September 1958 in defence of Dominic Behan; apparently a newspaper had linked him to subversive activities. Gilliam had raised the issue and David was making the case for Behan. He says that, firstly, the journalist seems to be confusing him with one of his brothers, Brendan or Paudge. Dominic Behan's jail sentences in Ireland were for strike offences, Thomson points out, 'he is a folk singer of international repute,' he continues. 'Yes, he sings what are called IRA ballads. But the ones written by Dominic are in fact anti-IRA ballads.' As evidence he points out irony in 'The Patriot Game':

Come all ye young rebels
And list while I sing,
Love of one's land is a terrible thing,
It banishes fear
With the speed of a flame,
And makes you all part
Of the Patriot's game

There's a letter to David in May 1956 from Dominic's more famous brother Brendan. Writing from Herbert Street, Dublin, he apologizes profusely for a phone call he had made to David the previous week, berating him and the BBC for sending 'the dough', as he called it, to his old address. David had produced *The Quare Fella* for radio. Behan concludes:

> But whoever's fault it was, you had acted most promptly and so had the other people in your department and I feel very low about this, and would be pleased if you could forgive me.
>
> Yours penitently,
> Brendan

By the late 1950s, Laurence Gilliam's Features Department was increasingly under scrutiny. Kate Whitehead describes the decline and eventual fall of Gilliam's administration. Senior management were suspicious of the department's relaxed atmosphere. The idea that people would be paid a salary and allowed to spend time having programme meetings, or general creative discussions, in the pub – and perhaps not return to the office at all, wasn't going to prevail. Another reason for disbanding it, she says, was the fact that their pioneering techniques were now well known in other departments. In their history of radio, John Snagg and Michael Barsley sum up the end for Gilliam, who received the honour Order of the British Empire only twenty years previously: 'Laurence, who planned on the grand scale, had been left with little to plan. It was therefore necessary to force upon him premature retirement. Gilliam *was* Features and it was necessary to topple him in advance, in order to break up his organisation.'*

Gilliam died in 1964 at the age of fifty-seven; MacNeice had passed away a year earlier, aged fifty-five. Eight years later, the Third Programme was gone, subsumed into BBC Radio Three. There remained, however, a link with Gilliam for the remainder of David's life through his daughter, Nina Hutchison (1943–94). She was a socialist and feminist who also had career as a community outreach and education officer in several London councils and the Greater London Council. She joined the socialist feminist group Big Flame and was involved in the Troops Out movement. This was during the period of the Labour Left's influence in local politics during the 1970s and 1980s, that Conservative power put an end to. During her life, Hutchison maintained an interest and regard for her father and his colleagues' legacy in BBC Radio. She was instrumental

* Snagge and Barsley, *Those Vintage Years*.

with Seamus Heaney in organizing the memorial evening for David Thomson in Dublin in February 1989.

After Gilliam's departure, David and his colleagues had to work with a more formal, managed system. In April 1964 David unsuccessfully proposed a programme where he would make a return journey to Nairn. The memo he wrote pitching the idea reveals his view then of his family background; he condemns his Uncle Robert, the ex Lord Chancellor, as an 'antediluvian patriarch'; recalls that he was romantically attached by legends like those of Culloden Moor; his liking for the townspeople who were 'a kind of escape from my own antique Presbyterian family'. He concludes: 'Would Third Programme send me to Nairn for about three weeks?'

For his production 'To Have and To Hold' in February 1969, a translation of *Haben* by Julius Hay (translated by Martina), David, with an eye for detail, engaged a Hungarian dancing teacher 'to advise the cast on traditional Hungarian dance steps'. Other programme-maker's housekeeping-type memos include a request to borrow a Uher tape recorder, the standard machine at the time, to travel to Ireland to record material for a programme about cats and their lore. He returns empty handed explaining that five contributors were not available, but that he would be going to Ireland on holiday that summer, 1969, and would complete the recordings then. He asks, modestly enough, for just two nights subsistence in Sligo and some taxi fares. He also wrote a letter before going to Dublin to Ted Furey, father of the Furey Brothers, in Claddagh Road, Ballyfermot: 'I wondered whether you and Séamus Ennis (if you can find him) would try out some cat music on the fiddle and uilleann pipes?' Nothing came of this, of course, because it looks like David was having his leg pulled by someone. He had apparently been told of a tune in the Irish tradition called 'The Cat's Keen for its Mother', but no such tune exists.

The BBC's audience research department analysed the transmitted programme in June 1969, a month after its broadcast. Their method was to ask a small sample of the audience and what they thought of the programme; what's now called a qualitative survey. Thomson's programme passed, but not with honours, receiving a reaction index of 62. The average for the first quarter of that year was 65. For a relatively specialist broadcast, it was a solid performance.

Some were repelled by the descriptions of brutality and cruelty to cats, which David had included.

MAYO: In County Mayo in the old time I heard my father say, they'd put a cat under a new boat, upturn the boat and close her in beneath it and let her die there before they went to launch the boat. The boat would be lucky that way.

The programme also explored happier traditions:

ICELAND: The expression Freyja Kettir in Icelandic – Freyja's cat – means the glad eye given by a woman. If she desires you she gives you the Cat of Freyja, the cat of the goddess of love and of the night, the most beautiful of the goddesses, the northern Venus, sister of Frey.

Listeners found it amusing and intriguing, and the Irish folk tales delightful. A 'psychic' atmosphere had been created, according to one; others found a preoccupation with horror that depressed them. A computer consultant comments that the programme has a 'sense of otherness', which must have flattered the producer.

There is warmth in all the correspondence between Thomson and his Irish contacts. One of these relationships that became another long friendship was with Seán Ó Súilleabháin. He was a colleague of Séamus Ó Duilearga and had a special talent for the cataloguing of folklore collected in the field. He was 'small in stature, self effacing, with a distinctive quivering voice'.* Ó Súilleabháin had concluded one of his letters to David with some practical news from Dublin: 'Guinness and spirits have jumped in price on account of a mini budget, and the publicans are clamouring for a still further increase. Bring a few extra pounds with you next time you come!'

During his BBC career, Thomson's left-leaning views on matters global were not dormant. The Vietnam War and the tacit support that America was receiving from the Labour government appalled him. He wrote to the Prime Minister, Harold Wilson, and received a lengthy, if anodyne reply from his private secretary on 3 February 1966: 'Mr Wilson has asked me to say that it has always been the policy of the Government to try and bring the tragic fighting in Vietnam to a conclusion by getting the parties round a conference table.'

In 1970 the BBC announced a new direction in a document, 'Broadcasting in the Seventies', which led to a restructuring of BBC Radio into Radios 1, 2, 3 and 4, a radical move, or 'division by brow', as it was called. It was a

* Briody, *The Irish Folklore Commission*.

response by the Corporation to the growing influence of television and the emerging independent radio sector. The Third Programme was gone, some of its programming would move the Radio 3 schedule and some to Radio 4. 'The outstanding creative achievement of BBC Radio will be abolished' claimed a letter to *The Times*.

To read in our digital age the reaction by staff to the BBC changes is quaintly fascinating. 'Sound broadcasting is in cataclysm; structures shift and change; new forces are at work,' proclaimed the Radio Writers Association in 1973. Staff at BBC was virtually in revolt. 'Broadcasting in the Seventies pays full regard to quantity of listening and to degree of appreciation, but no apparent regard to quality of listening,' said a trade union statement. But, of course, the world didn't end. Serious programming would be more 'on offer' than 'spoon fed', but remain in the schedules, as it does to this day.

David Thomson retired from the BBC in 1969, just as these changes were about to happen, although he contributed freelance for a period afterwards. The BBC had been generous to him, twice giving a year's sabbatical leave at half-pay, but he felt it was time to go. There was another significant factor in his decision; his hearing had declined significantly. He was fifty-five and about to become a full time writer and familiar face on the streets of Camden Town.

That same year his old friend and colleague, Bertie Rodgers died in Los Angeles, aged sixty. He had been elected a life member of the Irish Academy of Letters in 1951, to fill the vacancy left by the death of George Bernard Shaw, who died in November 1950. In 1968 Rodgers was awarded a life annuity of £100 by the Irish Arts Council as an acknowledgment of his distinction in letters. The Northern Ireland Arts Council had already honoured him. Though he'd died in California after emigrating there in 1966, he was buried in Loughgall, County Armagh, where he'd been a Presbyterian minister before his adventurous career change in 1946.

David contributed to a Radio 4 series in 1970 called *Whom the Gods Loved*, profiles of gifted people over the centuries. Franz Schubert was his choice. The programme begins atmospherically at a momentous event in music history, Beethoven's funeral in Vienna on 29 March 1827.

> READER: In the files on either side, from the head of the procession back to the hearse, were the torch bearers, thirty-six in number, consisting of musicians, and among them Herren Castelli, Czerny, David, Grillparzer, Lachner

and Schubert, all in funereal clothes with white roses and bunches of lilies tied to their arms with crepe, and with burning wax torches.

In his programme file, 'Characters and Notes on Them', David suggests to the producer, Graham Gauld, that Schubert must sound younger than anyone else in the programme, adding: 'He obviously had a lovable sense of humour. Even letters written when he was depressed could show where possible an ironical feeling against himself.' The programme conveys the elation felt by Schubert when after years of following Beethoven around Vienna and admiring from a distance, he finally gets to present some of his work to the great man, who later pronounced: 'Truly, in Schubert there dwells a divine spark.' Thomson, as a young man in Roscommon, would surely have heard Schubert's work sung in the drawing-room of Woodbrook House by his employer, Ivy Kirkwood.

David must have got carried away with expanding on the composer's life as curt notes from Gauld indicate it was 'eight pages too long, I fancy. Could you let me have some extensive cuts please?' Another piece of housekeeping followed when David queried the BBC 's offer of £80 for the Schubert script, asserting the fact that he had three adult and two children's books published at this stage. He looks for 90 Guineas, and then settles for £85.

Thomson's friend and early publisher, John Bunting, summed up his BBC career in a letter to a member of the Arts Council, Dame Veronica Wedgwood, in which he sought a grant for David. He described him as one of the better Third Programme feature producers in the BBC, maker of some brilliantly imaginative programmes. At the same time, his client 'wasn't too proud to tackle more hum-drum jobs for the BBC'. This made an enviable epitaph to a career. Dame Wedgewood replies, suggesting that the book does indeed sound promising, though her own efforts at securing grants for writers for historical subjects, she concedes, haven't been too successful lately. She ends with a gentle ageist note: 'Could you get someone with a younger and "with it" vintage?'

David Thomson was subsequently awarded £1000 by the Arts Council, a kickstart to his new life as a full-time writer.

7. Moral Candour, Fiction and 'Fiction'

In September 1961 a passenger ship, SS *Uganda* was on a voyage from Mombasa to Marseilles. The passengers in Cabin 88 was a married man with young children, a BBC producer and published writer, who had a mind that brimmed – and wandered. He wrote in his notebook: 'Continental stars by the swimming pool ... Lolita, the beautiful English slim one comes (why?) near me at the pool and says your cigarette will get all wet from people splashing it ...'

The Guardian's literary editor W. L Webb observed in his obituary for David Thomson that 'He was loved for a sort of valorous vulnerability, which is partly moral candour, partly the courage to pursue insights that come from the gift or disability of having fewer layers of psychic insulation than most of us.'

David always carried notebooks, as we know. A particularly candid series of these writings he gave the ironic name, 'Diary of a Madman', which was taken from a book of short stories of the same title by Nikolai Gogol, the Ukrainian-born writer. Thomson's diary entries were mostly written during the 1960s, when he was in psychiatric care. These dreams, fantasies, humour, and streams of consciousness share much with his fiction works. On examination, these books are not really fiction at all but David Thomson letting us into his life, with only a thin veil of disguise.

These diaries are often blunt. In one entry he sums up some colleagues in the BBC as having 'minds like housing estates'. In 1966 he describes attending an anti-motorway meeting in Camden Town, where he's semi-detached from proceedings, but 'really appreciated the manic state which allows me to see people vividly in the caricatures and excitement that I felt for strangers as a boy'.

The 1961 ship's diary continued:

Tuesday 5th September. In Red Sea, near Port Sedan

Mermaid is unfortunately – luckily – English by attitude and daresay parents, Kenya coffee plantations – or worse. But beautiful blonde dark shoulder hair, perfect body, agile swimmer, delicate (muslin?) white blouse and cherry coloured short skirt, during day, long brown bare legs, sandals swimming suit, not bikini, but very good pattern showing small breasts of same colour as cherry. Last night's unplanned encounter after Aden was nice and natural and good for us both, me fully dressed, first class, regulation tie ... on swimming pool bench where light is good reading Tolstoy – saw her swimming with handsome young man and older man (father?)

– Is he your husband – or boyfriend?

(Laugh)

– 'I'm not married. Don't you like swimming?'

Thomson was probably only expressing what many other men might dream of – an encounter with a potent young woman. He was recovering, of course, from his breakdown in Dar-es-Salaam, and was travelling back to home and his job after what Martina referred to as the 'East Africa episode'. He later identified the 'mermaid' as a Miss Valerie Tagham, a student at Exeter University. 'Swam away beautifully, violently – my last words with her. Forever, I hope. Complications too much. But she must be going at least to Marseilles and what can I do? And now she has reversed last night's natural encounter – perhaps parents worried her off. Perhaps my evident madness now frightens her.' The remainder of this notebook contains David's thoughts on the repertoire of the ship's jazz band and their interpretation of Louis Armstrong.

This diary resumes again several years later, written in another exotic location. David had been given sabbatical leave from the BBC and took the family to Greece: once to Spetsai and on another occasion to Paros. Martina Thomson remembers it as exotic and primitive in a time before mass tourism. But the diaries tell a different story, where demons were everywhere. In a 1965 notebook in Paros he reflects on mood swings, his BBC job, and life after fifty-one and how he might write again: 'Now I take a long time over each book, whatever the subject and the method. What shall I do with the rest of my life?'

In the entry of 10 July 1965, he is disturbed, but articulate and candid:

> Early mornings are worst for gloom, though it's nothing as bad as depression in London. But it has a very distressing part – can't confide in M or talk closely especially in the evenings and am separated from her not only physically, pitifully, regretfully behind the glass I have put up, her beauty wasted on me, her sun brown body. Wasted and secretly loved by me.

In July 1966, when he is again in psychiatric care, he picks up a theme from his childhood, this time in relation to Taffy, the horse he kept at Edingthorpe:

> Every handling of Taffy, and especially grooming and harnessing, picking out hooves etc., kept me in a constant state of sexual excitement. Our last drive to take him back to Trimmingham was one of the most enjoyable I can remember. This reminds me that on a summer high mania 2 or 3 years ago I went to horse shows instead of looking at women.

He describes a mixed-emotions afternoon where Martina realized that there was another woman somewhere in the background when she visited Halliwick with their children that summer, a woman called Anna, who he describes as dominating the atmosphere in her absence, creating a feeling of 'melancholy' as they all sat on the lawn.

He reveals in the entry for 5 June 1966 that a friend had described him as 'sex mad Thomson'. But David is almost mocking himself when he writes: 'Fortunately for everyone else the harem is living in [my] head and is likely to stay there till I get depressed again when all its beautiful inmates will wither away, the sad faded beauties will be ignored by me or even physically revolt me.' Halliwick had brought him interesting experiences, an attempt to get him to join a painting class, encounters with other patients and detached observations of others: We get a picture of a disturbed young man, a plasterer and decorator who apparently wanted to become a scene painter for the stage and had a fascination for St Paul's Cathedral, which he was allowed out to visit. David describes sympathetically how the man seemed to get obsessed with detail: 'He said a certain rack of picture postcards spoiled the symmetry of one part of the interior.'

Then David was discharged. 'I am to be released from the Halliwick today – this open prison which I half like.' The diary continues that summer of 1966, when the family went to Edingthorpe:

> Two crises de nerfs since we came to the country. The worst was when Tim knocked over a glass of water on to the supper table with a crash. I looked at the glass on its side and at pools of water of various shapes on the oilcloth and had a fit of trembling – imagine my face must have been contorted too. Benjamin laughed when he saw me, but afterwards told M he 'laughed and cried'.

These kind of incidents, and Martina's 'jealousy' crises, seem to have been outweighed by the love and regard that she and the three boys had for him. He tried unsuccessfully to resume writing, describing his feelings 'as if mind and body had suddenly switched over to a lower key'.

David discontinued 'Diary of a Madman' in the last years of his life. But an entry in Martina's diary two months after his death refers to David's equine musings -something had rubbed off from 'Diary of a Madman' in her own thoughts. She describes being in Regents Park, at a horse parade they used to watch as a family: 'Suddenly I saw horses as you saw them as girls. The harnesses prevented me seeing their buttocks, but I loved their heads, manes, chests, front legs – their lively movements when trotting. I was overcome by the sexiness of all these girl horses in this variety of kind, size and colour.'

David's mental lows did sometimes bring comfort to others. When his colleague in Ireland, Séamus Delargy, wrote to David in December 1961, not long after David's African episode, expressing sympathy, Delargy reveals something about himself. 'I must say that I was worried when I was told of your illness, because I had suffered a good deal from the same ailment and I know how distressing it can be. Thank God, you and your wife and the children will have a happy Christmas together now that you are restored to health.'

David also shared his mental troubles with another friend, Roger Wilton, who lived in Gosport, Hampshire. Wilton is one of those old-fashioned long expressive letter writers that the Thomson papers are full of. In December 1982 he brings David news. His wife had just 'jettisoned' him and gone to live in Canada and work with the Eskimo people. 'I absolutely hate being on my own night and day, but am lucky having got myself referred to a special clinic – dreadful implications – which deals with 'nutters' like me who are driven to introversion and the like by circumstances beyond their control.'

And Thomson's mental volatility had one particular side effect. The musings in 'Diary of a Madman' were an impetus for and gave 'a hint of sulphur' to his fiction works. The result wasn't always successful, however. An incomplete manuscript 'Janine', among his Edinburgh papers, written in Paros in 1965, opens with a surreal scene as the heroine wakes up in a strange apartment in Paris in early morning, not sure where she was the night before. As she looks over the balcony, a troupe of horses appears out of the fog. They were bay farm horses and their numbers seemed endless. 'She was enthralled by their grace and strength. Well fed and tended, in the prime of their life, their emergence out of the silent fog was inexplicable and it was not until the sound of their hooves had died away in the distance that everyday life began to invade the street.' Thomson's descriptive ability with horses is familiar, of course: 'a stallion arching its powerful neck, raising its braided tail like a horse in a painting by Géricault'.

The draft stays in the National Library of Scotland, as does 'Matthew Pirie', also written in Greece, in 1962. A letter from his friend Philip O'Connor dismisses the 'Matthew Pirie' draft bluntly. 'I don't much like it. You haven't the handrails of a concrete story as you had in the other novels.'

David Thomson's fiction was more successful when it was set closer to home – and closer to the bone. It may have been more uncomfortable for the family, but he succeeded in getting three – heavily autobiographical – fiction works published, *Daniel*, *A Break in the Sun* and *Dandiprat's Days.* All were about David Thomson. In a notebook in 1978 he even referred to his fiction as 'fiction'. His son Ben refers to *A Break in the Sun* as 'Oh that one where he goes mad in Africa?'

Barrie & Rockliff published *Daniel* in 1962. Daniel is a nineteen-year-old misfit, an upper-middle class, chronically non-competitive young man, whose career is a succession of odd jobs. His life centres on a St John's Wood pub where the landlady, Jessie, is fond of him and is understanding – and sexually permissive. He has contemplated suicide because of the vacancy of his own life. In Berlin at the same time there's Susanna, the daughter of a wealthy but intellectual manufacturer. She's Jewish by birth, but not religion. She is similarly isolated, but for a better reason; the Nazis have come to power. On one occasion, Susanna's father explains to his daughter that he cannot repair her doll because the dolls' hospital is next door to the storm troopers' barracks.

The novel opens on Shrove Tuesday in 1933; the night after the Reichstag in Berlin is burnt. When the book ends, the atomic bomb has been dropped on Hiroshima.

The *Times Literary Supplement* in June 1962 recommended it be read for its humanity. Louis MacNeice, Thomson's friend and colleague, of course, enthused: 'Daniel is a splendid creation, a kind of holy clown, engaged on a blundering pilgrimage towards love, which at last he finds with Susanna. The whole book, with its wide sweep that takes in slapstick, tragedy and idyll, is both refreshingly new and true to the world we live in.'

A Break in the Sun, published in 1965, comes directly out of David's East Africa experience, detailed in the last chapter of this book. The *TLS* commented: 'Alive and walking from the first page to the last. It is funny but not satirical, individual but not private, philosophical but not a *roman a these* ... it has a spontaneous and unexpected quality rare in a story that is so well constructed, sophisticated and qualified with irony.'

The novel continues the story of the same Daniel Cullen of *Daniel*, now several years older, who loses his sanity in Africa and then regains it. Daniel has more than a passing resemblance to David Thomson: He works for a broadcaster called The Great Auk; he's a producer, but television rather than radio. He was born in Quetta in 1914. His father was in the Indian army before being sent to the front during the First World War. While in Africa and his mind is running riot, he imagines he can see beyond Mount Kilimanjaro across Madagascar to the land of his birth. He keeps a journal where 'his heart and his head get mixed up'. He writes to his wife to 'forgive him for the unfaithfulness to come'.

He is naturally very intellectual and muses on the connection between sexual desire and creativity. Sexual impotence had made him depressed in the past, but in Africa he acquired a feeling of sexual strength, which has fired him up: 'Was it to do with the heat of Africa, with lack of sleep and food? And what connection was there between sexual desire and imaginative power, creative energy and the rest? Periods of celibacy had always destroyed his mental and spiritual powers, had induced in him irritable pettiness, meanness and a lust for money.'

He is assigned to shoot a documentary on one country's independence movement. For one reason and another it never happens. Female company arrives, first with bizarre results, then with fulfilment of a kind. First, he imagines the woman he's sleeping with in Dar-es-Salaam is Susanna, his first love, and after a nightmare he's convinced he has to save her from the Nazis. This

Susanna is the name of the woman in his first novel *Daniel* who bore an uncanny resemblance to Martina. In *A Break in the Sun* Martina is portrayed as Penelope, his wife back in London. In fact, David daringly uses phrases from actual letters written by Martina at the height of the real 'East Africa episode' in letters from Penelope. 'I dreamt you loved a girl and the room was for her now ... I saw you carrying two packets of lentils for her supper.' He has Penelope signing the letters 'à toi', Martina's favourite sign-off. In the end, the scenario is almost identical to the Thomsons own story in 1961 – reuniting in Paris. So an impossible caveat for a David Thomson novel would be, 'Any resemblance to persons living or dead is purely coincidental'.

Dandiprat's Days, published in 1983, was David Thomson's last fiction work to appear in print. Dandiprat is another character whose name begins with a 'D', just like Daniel. Dandiprat is also a person from a well-to-do background, who suffers from eccentricity and precarious mental health. He spends much of the period of the book, a diary, in his 'home from home', a psychiatric hospital somewhere in London. Like his creator, he has a writing desk in an elegant period house close to a major railway line. He is also a civil servant. He is unlike his author in one respect; he has never had a relationship with a woman, though he craves it, now in his mid fifties.

David's study, the front room of 22 Regent's Park Terrace, Camden Town, in 2013.

He has been prescribed Tryptizol by his doctor and the effects are alarming: 'Last night was the worst night. The devil came. It is four in the morning now and I'm safe for a while at the desk in my study. My hand and even my head are shaking, teeth chattering even though the room is warm. What can I do? He will come again tomorrow.'

Dandiprat has contemplated suicide, in a canal – another reference close to home in Camden Town. But Dandiprat is a struggler, who is inspired by beauty. On one occasion he's very eloquently describing the joy that the garden in the hospital gives him. The flowerbeds and the way they are arranged starts to fascinate him; the Thomson familiarity with plants. He describes aubrietia, as 'purple rock cress as my mother used to call it'. (Aubrietia is a flowering plant, named after Claude Aubriet, a French flower painter.) Another meditation on time and memory follow:

> So now with the past and present both physically present in the same scene, renewed by nature as richly as before, I live without the present. I reach for the past. In spite of the sleeping bombs they give me at bedtime – blue one end and red the other – I wake at six and take this exercise book from my bedside closet.

Dandiprat is discharged and while in his local pub meets Virginia, the woman who will transform his life. He becomes very attracted to her, and then she disappears. He mentions all this to his psychiatrist, Dr Psex. He understands – or imagines – that the psychiatric advice is that he needs to consort with Virginia, because 'virginity' is his problem. This play on words is typical of the book's humour.

When he eventually finds her, she's working for the council with a brush and wheelbarrow. He 'rescues' her, putting the barrow in the back seat of his Bentley. A relationship of sorts begins. Dandiprat cruises the streets, looking for her at her 'knocking off time'. There are complications: she's a single mother, a little unpredictable and not that stable – like him. And there's another man lurking in her life. The fact that she's about half Dandiprat's age is the least of his problems. But Dandiprat is smitten:

> Monday
>
> My whole life has changed. The very leaves of the trees outside my window are individually beautiful, each one distinguishable in unison with the rest which I used to gaze at as one cloud of green.

On their first date, he reads the Bible to her, from the Book of Ruth. As he wonders how he ended up reading the bible to her, he's putting it aside then she says, 'Don't – I want to see what you get from it.' The night of revelation continues for Dandiprat when Virginia declares, inspired by Ruth, 'I have washed and anointed myself. Spread your skirt over me.' Dandiprat doesn't quite know how to react. But Thomson is subtle, avoiding probably unnecessary explicitness: 'Her gentle touch made my touch gentle, and we lay face to face without speaking; my first delight was her skin against mine. The delights, which ensued, are unspeakable and it is not necessary to write them down.'

The relationship continues tumultuously and with a high degree of uncertainty, as Virginia keeps disappearing and reappearing around North London, till on the last page he concedes he's lost her and declares with resignation: 'She will lie at the feet of another Boaz and another and each will spread his skirt over her.' He ends the book in scholarly fashion, putting his own spin on a verse inspired by the ancient poet from the second century BC, Callimachus:

I mourn for Ruth who is Virginia, who is my Crethis.
Crethis, their first in tale or play,
Sorely the Samian maidens weep,
Their pretty task mate, prattler gay,
Sleeps, as must they, her fated sleep.

Another translation from Callimachus also echoes Dandiprat's experience:

The Samian virgins used often to play,
With Crethis the witty, the pleasant, the gay,
But now when they seek her she cannot be found,
Their sportive companion sleeps here underground.

In a review in *British Book News* in January 1984, Bryn Caless called *Dandiprat's Days* a book about the mind's twilight and said that reading a David Thomson novel was not to be undertaken by the lazy or indifferent: 'He has always been a writer who challenges, bemuses and teases his readers into greater participation (and therefore greater fulfilment) in the making of a story.'

In 1965 David wrote the narration for a radio programme called 'Lunacy', and subtitled 'Legend and fact about mental illness from the early days of Christianity to the nineteenth century.' It begins in County Kerry, on the road between Tralee and Dingle, in a valley called Gleann na nGealt, the 'valley of the lunatics', where it was said that long ago every person of unsound mind would find their way to this valley if they were left to themselves. Peig Sayers and Tadhg Scanlon then provide local accounts of this. 'And everyone who lives in the Dingle Peninsula is familiar with tradition about this mysterious place,' the narrator says.

A year later, David, back in the Halliwick Hospital, is making a plea on behalf of modern sufferers and his fellow patients. Writing in 'Diary of a Madman', he expresses a frustration that must be felt by countless people who have been treated for mental illness:

> What I find most difficult to bear is the assumption that everything one did before incarceration is a symptom of 'mental illness'. Visits to Covent Garden, new friendships there, the buying or picking of flowers, my wish to buy a horse, stem not from the heart but from a diseased mind. I, and my fellow patients in this place, are nothing but containers for pills, which make us, feel this, or behave like that.

But Thomson could somehow banish these feelings, restore equilibrium, and start afresh with another episode of his life. In his case, the impulse was to forge on, seeking fulfilment through the medium of radio, and also by renewing his lifelong urge to express himself with words.

Folklore, tradition and old beliefs, particularly about the animal kingdom, were a great part of his writing career. The exploration of this world brought him back to Ireland many times.

8. Seal and Hare Uncovered

It was 10 August 1947. Two radio producers, an ex-IRA man and a famous uilleann piper are taking in the atmosphere at Puck Fair in Killorglin, County Kerry. The ceremonial wild goat is being hoisted high over the street to preside over the goings on. One of the BBC men has a diary: 'I sat on top of the recording car during the proceedings, and the public sat on Bertie's [Rodgers] and Séamus Ennis's car and covered them with cow dirt off their boots. Terrific consumption of Guinness.' The diarist was David Thomson's colleague Jack Dillon.

The ex-IRA man and BBC guide was Ernie O'Malley, born in Castlebar in 1897, and one of the central figures in the Irish War of Independence and Civil War. The literary quality of his books and his career after the political conflicts distinguish him from other IRA men who also penned memoirs of the times. He led a colourful life, gave up medicine since returning to study it after the Civil War, emigrated to the US, and spent time in Taos, New Mexico, and Mexico City. He became known in literary and artistic circles in New York during the Depression era. He married an American, Helen Hooker, in 1935, though they separated in 1950. He published his most famous book, *On Another Man's Wound*, in 1936. He had at least one other great claim to fame: he knew John Ford and advised John Wayne during the making of *The Quiet Man*.

In an article in *The Irish Times* in 1996 John McGahern, a friend and admirer of Thomson, described *On Another Man's Wound* as 'the one classic work to have emerged directly from the violence that led to independence'. On this 1947 summer journey, the diary describes O'Malley as 'A tremendous asset on the trip, especially in Kerry and the west, where a lot of the chaps he's fought with came from (always make full use of your prepositions!)'

There's an almost casual diary entry amid the descriptions of meals and quality of accommodation about one of Ireland's literary legends: 'Visited Peig Sayers in convent hospital, the queen of the Blaskets. Very beautiful, very old storyteller. A story concerning a man she married that she'd never met before. Ate mutton pies at Begley's, a Dingle speciality (not recommended) with Joe Daly of Dunquin, a folklorist.'

The group visits Carna, where a local priest, not recognizing O'Malley, talks about his past exploits and says he had heard that he had, 'gone over to the arts'. O'Malley brings David on his first visit to the Aran Islands. They then stopped at Burrishoole, County Mayo, close to Achill Island where Ernie O'Malley lived at that time. On 19 August O'Malley took ill and the BBC men continued without their new friend. The diary describes how very sad they all were to leave him. They continue to old Thomson haunts; first Frenchpark, where he had been a tutor for a brief period, and then to Boyle and Carrick-on-Shannon, where of course he had lived for ten years and where he now becomes very nostalgic over pints in Lowe's bar. Jack Dillon later gets a dose of food poisoning in Dublin, whereupon he is reminded by Thomson: 'I suppose you realize that when you go back everyone will tell you how lucky you were to go on this trip?'

We get another glimpse of the BBC working environment from a letter David wrote in September, following that Irish excursion, to Louis MacNeice, who was in India at the time. It was 1947, and India was in the turmoil of gaining its independence.

> We have now filtered back from Ireland, one by one. And of course nobody realised we'd been away, which is always so provoking. You do realize, don't you, that when you come back with your eyes stained with kohl and your teeth red with betel, or the other way around, they'll say 'have you being doing any shows lately, Louis?'.

David Thomson used his BBC work to kick-start his writing on several occasions – a privilege he and others enjoyed from their employer. His travels in Ireland had already produced the programme, 'Songs of the Seals'. He didn't leave it there and began drafting a manuscript based on his research. He was then delighted to get a letter in March 1952, when he was thirty-eight, from John Bunting, of Turnstile Press, who would remain a friend for the rest of his life: 'We are all most interested in the synopsis you sent us, which I think looks like it would make a delightful book and one we could sell as well as enjoy.'

David wrote to Bunting in August agreeing to his suggestion of a change of approach. He would now write the book from the personal point of view, to avoid 'preaching', as he called it. He was working through a literary agent, Pearl, Pollinger and Higham. Turnstile commissioned a reader's report from Nora Kershaw Chadwick, a noted Celtic scholar, who remembered being told stories of the Blasket Islands by Dr Robin Flower. 'In view of the highly specialised topic,' she reported on David's efforts, 'his treatment is the best possible one.' She then refers to the fact that Thomson doesn't know the Irish language: It thus lacks a flavour that it might have had, but she says 'David Thomson's fault in this is a good one, because he never rings false or attempts to reproduce anything he is not certain of.'

Tim Dee wrote in 2012 that while Thomson dealt with the changing lifestyle of Hebridean islanders, such as the arrival of cookers and televisions, 'none of this is done with the patronizing sentimentality of the romantic intellectual wishing to collect stone-age characters and stone-age beliefs'. He quotes a passage from the beginning of *The People of the Sea* that captures what he calls Thomson's 'extraordinary sensuous intelligence'. David is remembering his childhood in Nairn in the 1920s, and the farm, Sandwood, that he loved to visit and occasionally work in:

> Romance was made of the shadows and the wooden posts, the chains and buckets, the dark shapes hanging from the rafters, the bins of brown linseed cake, the dung and straw and hay, the steamy warmth, soft flanks and bony hips, warm udders, some with teats that were good to touch, some scabby or misshapen, the taste of the hot froth of new milk, the slow eyes of cattle and horses, the rhythmic munching, the coughing and the shuffling of the byre and stable.*

* *Archipelago*, Winter 2012.

During research, David wrote to Seán Ó Suillebháin asking was it true that there was a man in Killeaney on Inis Mór whose wife was never seen. One day there was no smoke from the chimney, he was found dead in one bed and in another the skeleton of a seal: 'Do you know anything about this or is it one of Pat Mullen's inventions?'

The People of the Sea is the narrative of a practical journey around Ireland and Scotland to delve into the legends and lore of seals, the borderline world between animal and human. Imagination and fact are intertwined, as in the best of Thomson's work.

He begins the book in his childhood in Nairn. He heard talk about a local woman, Mrs Carnoustie, who was said to be deformed. His mother's cousin, La, spoke of the woman's characteristics in an unusual way; her arms apparently only came down a little below her elbows. They were flattish, like flippers. To add to the mystery, the woman always wore a long black dress, shiny and fastened at the collar. David's mother questioned this account, saying that everyone's dress in those days came to the ground. The answer she got was 'not as much as hers did'.

People said the woman's mother was a seal. Her father had met a woman on a beach somewhere in Scotland, but she was a seal posing as a woman. They married and had a baby that was half-woman half-seal. It grew up to be Mrs Carnoustie. Or so the story went. She never bathed in the sea in case she'd reveal her true identity; she walked slowly because her feet were connected and stuck out sideways.

Then Thomson returns to *terra firma*, and the conversation takes a practical turn when he asked was Mrs Carnoustie one of 'those selchie folk'.

> 'No dearie, no, it's nothing but an old wifie's tale.'
>
> 'Is La an old wifie?'
>
> 'Indeed, how dare you say such things about Miss Charmers?'

Thomson sees a parallel between these two worlds of imagination and reality and his own life in Nairn. The people he met on his milk round belonged more to the former because of their earthiness. As his cart rattled along the street, he felt he was one with the town, then as he mingled with the other drivers, his accent betrayed him. He called it 'living two lives'.

The People of the Sea and its exploration of belief, with its encounters like scenes from a Synge play, continues in Munster when David teams up with Séamus Delargy. On the road between Kenmare and Killarney, Thomson catches sight of the famous lakes after a red deer has caused them to stop the car. The land was 'sodden and green and brown, smelling to me of the days of my childhood'. He has an interesting reflection, saying that the sight of the blue of the sea at Kenmare Bay had an effect on the two travellers, a hint of the trouble both men shared:

> But the sudden blue flash of the sea as we turned a bend in the hills above Kenmare Bay was a shock that brought us both out of the grey mood that had sat on us in Cork, in spite of the quays and whiskey, in spite of the ships from Stavanger and Cardiff and the Clyde. We were in shadow, but the sun was on the sea. And again, still more brightly and as sudden, we saw the sunset over Ballinskelligs Bay.

In Chapter 4 Thomson has arrived in North Mayo. Walking to his destination on the Erris peninsula, he comes across a stone cairn at the side of the road, and a story unfolds. A man, Michael the Ferry, greets him, asks where he's from, but guessing he was from England. For the man, England is a strange place where they 'burn the dead', a practice he can't countenance. He had been there to work at harvests several times, where he knew a man once whose wife had died, though she was a 'young, strong' woman. 'But didn't she die, and will you believe this – didn't he have her burned by fire. And he did love her, I believe.'

On the sea later, Michael the Ferry tells Thomson of the role seals play in judging the tides. If a seal is not doing well against the tide – and they're great swimmers, then you know not to take a boat out. But local belief was that seals are even more important as lifesavers. People knew that killing a seal was bad luck, so they never harmed one. Five men in their currach disappeared at sea once, and the feeling locally was that the belief had failed them – they had ignored the signs from the seals. Michael the Ferry takes delight at a gathering in the pub in telling the end of the story and how the fishermen were saved, having nearly died from exposure, after a seal alerted a lifeboat in Killybegs, sixty miles to the north, across Sligo Bay. The man on watch at the coastguard station heard the roaring of a seal:

> 'Twas no usual way in that place and twas no usual way the seal was roaring either, but it did go on and on and on close about the shore, from one end to

the other of the coastguard's place, until the watchman made sure there was something wrong and he watching the seal swim up and down before him.'

The story unfolds, the old men murmur their recollections and the stranger from BBC in London with the thick spectacles and the 'English' accent is taking it all in and noting everything, including the fact that the others in the room except him knew the story well, but were eager to hear every detail again. As the night wore on, and 'black drinks were had', Thomson was struck by the body language of some of the men, particularly how one, who hardly spoke, used an ash plant to strike the floor when one said something that sparked his memories. Then there was a man who spoke differently to the rest, particularly when he used English. He had the same accent, but his words and phrases were chosen with care. Thomson was not surprised when the man told him later that he had spent twenty years in the British army.

One of the things Thomson captures in this book is the whole manner of storytelling, the procedure, the protocol, the wait, and the person composing themselves as if to begin a speech. The listeners know the story, but they want to hear it again. This importance of the telling, and the power of repetition, were comically observed in the modern era by Pat Shortt in *Killinaskully*. Before the character Dan Clancy begins to tell a story, his friend Jimmy would say to the assembled, 'He tells this lovely,' before going on to steal Dan's best lines before he can say them.

Eamon Kelly took up a not dissimilar theme in paying tribute to David Thomson in 1989. He recalled his and Delargy's visit to Waterville in *The People of the Sea,* to Tadhg Treacy's house where Seán Sweeney the storyteller was present. Kelly, no stranger to the storyteller's art himself, talked about the importance 'that sort of ritualistic time, when the people in the kitchen joined in the conversation with the storyteller, setting the mood for that magic moment that's going to come, the moment when the story begins'. His point was that Thomson the 'outsider' had captured this.

Thomson hears stories of the warnings given by women who travelled the roads in those times. There was a particular tale that has a moral about human vanity. The man in the tale has his eye on a particular seal; a white one that he thinks will make the 'finest waistcoat in north Mayo'. He does the deed and the story proceeds with a visit by one such woman, where she thanks him for his kindness to her over the years. Then she notices the dead seal. She enquires as to whether he had killed the creature himself and he says he had. 'I'm afraid,' she says, 'there is harm in that for you.' A year later the man went one day to work on the bog and was found dead the next, by the same woman who had made the prophesy.

As Thomson is leaving, Michael the Ferry tells him about seals' role in bereavement, and respect for the dead. As they pass the beach beside the graveyard, he tells him that his father had seen sixty seals there on the day of his own father's burial.

> 'What happened,' says David.
>
> 'I'll tell you next time you come', says the local man.

Seamus Heaney wrote an introduction to the 2001 edition. He said the reader must go on a journey where disbelief is suspended:

> David Thomson's achievement is pre-eminently stylistic; his writing combines a feel for the 'this-worldness' of his characters' lives with an understanding of the 'other-worldness' they keep a place for in their consciousness. Which is a way of saying that the stylistic achievement depends upon a deep imaginative sympathy. What could have been a matter of fieldwork being written up into a casebook becomes a matter of memory and its contents being liberated into a new and transfigured pattern.*

At the Royal Irish Academy commemoration in 1989, the poet Nuala Ní Dhomhnaill took up this thought in Thomson's work, the fascination with attributing human traits to creatures. She recalled being in a classroom with third-year honours students at Maynooth University and reading a piece from the writing of Peig Sayers about a seal that rises from the waves to verbally challenge a man who is about to kill it. She quoted the creature's words then asked the class repeatedly: '*Cad dúirt an rón le Mac Uí Shé?*' She said she eventually realized it wasn't that the students didn't understand the question in Irish; it was that they didn't understand the concept, because as far as they were concerned seals don't talk. 'But seals do talk in this book,' she said, because Thomson had the advantage of what she called 'an Aboriginal mind-set'. Her conclusion about the power of belief was: 'You don't have to go to Australia. We have it here at home and we shouldn't be embarrassed by it.'

---

* *The People of the Sea* (Canongate Classics, 2001).

During his early years in the BBC, David was introduced one day to one of Features' programme contributors. The men took to each other, discovering a shared interest in folklore. The relationship became one of the most productive of David's career. George Ewart Evans (1909-88) was a native of Abercynon, a mining town in South Wales. He served in the RAF during the war and then settled in Suffolk, where he set about recording the dialect and customs of his neighbours. In the early 1970s he and David embarked on a book project, *The Leaping Hare.* It was an excursion into the lore surrounding the animal that was published by Faber in 1972. Ewart Evans' daughter, Sue, remembers the collaboration as a teenager. She confirms that her father soon became a close friend of David Thomson and was much helped by him in the early days of his writing work. David's collaboration with George and the airing of their work on the Third Programme was instrumental in getting Ewart Evans's work known to a larger public. David showed Ewart Evans how to use an early tape recorder, called a Mighty Midget, enabling him to make recordings of old farm workers whose memory stretched back to the nineteenth century. These recordings are at the British Library Sound Archive, and are also now available online.

Sue Ewart Evans's elder sister Mary also remembers David Thomson, in 1964, arriving to see George, bringing a huge bunch of orchids for their mother, Florence. Orchids were a rare flower in the 1960s. 'This present went down in our family history as an example of someone being on a wonderful extravagant and generous high.'

Most of Sue's memories of David come from 1967 on, when she became David Gentleman's partner, and moved next door to the Thomsons in Camden Town. The seasoned drinker introduced her to the tradition of a pint of Guinness with a 'chaser' of Irish whiskey, later teasing her for drinking it too quickly. Most of their meetings, she recalls, were in pubs or at rather boozy parties.

David and Martina visited George and Florence in Norfolk towards the end of George's life in late 1987. Martina told Sue when they returned that no one had answered the door and they had to let themselves in. George was very deaf and Florence had advanced senility. 'She was a Quaker and non-drinker, and I felt she always had a disapproving look when David was mentioned. Martina was aware of this and we often joked about it.' Thomson and Ewart Evans shared poor hearing from middle age. Both died in 1988.

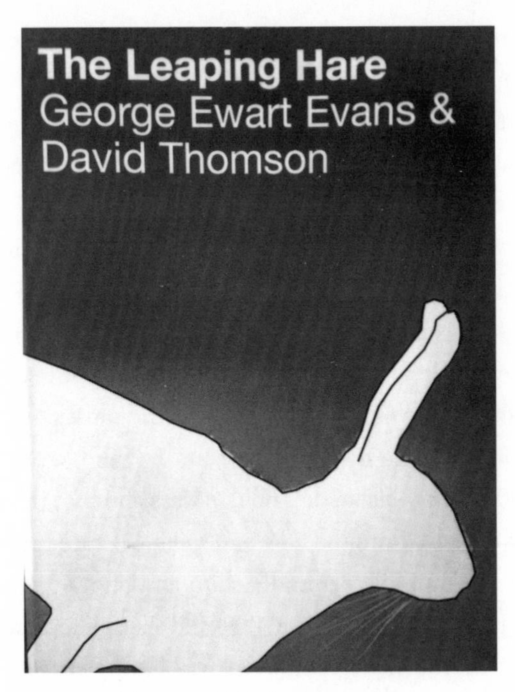

The cover of The Leaping Hare.

The Leaping Hare is a mystery story from the natural world. Thomson and Ewart Evans reveal the hare's mythical, other-worldly relationship to humans, the creature's apparent sense and sensibility. They discuss the hare with folklorists, naturalists, and writers – and, of course, gamekeepers, who tend to offer an unsentimental curiosity about the animal. No creature in the countryside, they say, is the focus of so many different points of view as the hare.

The Leaping Hare examines the erroneous belief that the hare is hermaphrodite or that hares change gender from year to year, or even month to month. It was said also that a female hare escaped from the Ark and was drowned, leaving only one hare. So God gave him the power to bear children. The 'female one month, male the next' belief derives, the authors think, from a concept expressed in many religions and myths in which the god or the perfect human being is spiritually and physically hermaphrodite, as Adam was before Eve was taken out of his body and made into a separate person.

Hares and rabbits do not fraternize, apparently. And hares will not graze on land used by rabbits. as the other creatures make the grass seem foul, the same way that cattle do not like pasture that geese have been on. The hare has an uncanny instinct to try and race aircraft (before security fences). Is the animal doing this to take on a challenge? The authors conclude that in using its speed to compete with the aeroplane, it's demonstrating one of its strongest instincts of self-expression, not unlike dolphins insisting on swimming alongside boats for miles.

The Scottish lore in the book is evidence of Thomson's side of the collaboration. The Scottish native *lepus* is the mountain hare. He recalls firstly seeing the butchers' shops in Nairn well stocked with lifeless ones. He realized that the mountain hare's white winter coat was a liability without snow. On Culloden Moor without snowfall, he observes, the hare is the most conspicuous creature. Writing this section he uses the third person, 'he' and 'a Scottish informant'. This person would borrow his uncle's field glasses and bicycle out to the moors, usually alone, and observe both the hare and that now rare bird, the capercaillie. The hare's 'unhurried jumps' reminded him of a horse smoothly cantering. Sometimes when it ran on level ground it would seem like a puff of smoke rising and falling, blown by the wind. Thomson was having private lessons in Latin then from a minister of the Episcopal Church, hence this imagery: 'When we tried to imagine the Holy Ghost we thought of the white hare. The mysterious sin against the Holy Ghost was to kill a white hare.'

Yet Thomson can deal in a matter-of-fact way with the killing of hares. He recalls a postman from Sally Grove, County Roscommon, who carried on the tradition of carrying a small stone with him, a round pebble from the seashore that could fit neatly into the palm of a hand. He always had this stone with him as he travelled round with the letters. There are echoes of the seal experience in another hunter's account, in which the hare is trapped in a 'hare hole': 'Have you ever heard a hare dyin in a hare-hole? You'd never suffer one again when you're living. The mournful cry of them is frightening. She cries like a child. You'd never set a hare hole again.'

In the closing chapter, 'And now Good Day to You, Sir Hare', the authors lament the modern disbelief in myths or their value. They conclude that as long as we possess some of the hare's apparent attributes – unpredictability, its occasional 'jumping over the head of reason', its sharpness, its seasonal abandon, and its frequent stupidity – the myth of the hare will not be entirely dead. Seamus Heaney would return to this theme after Thomson's passing. *The Leaping Hare*'s authors had left food for his imagination, as they concluded: 'But we have not been able to hold the creature completely. It has always been able to turn suddenly, to execute its *mazes*, to accelerate or swerve out of the neat grid of classification, to disappear through an opening, its *smile* or *meuse*, which the classifier had neither noticed nor suspected.'

Tim Dee, a writer and radio producer like David Thomson, speculates as to what drew him so much in his work to the natural world. He thinks it was the fact that animals don't know who they are; they don't care, unlike humans on the other hand, where consciousness of who we are imposes a type of tyranny that Thomson liked escaping from. He thinks David had a desire to lose his ego, to lose his identity, in the same way he feels, he may have found alcohol a 'journey away from himself'.

9. Man and Fox

The natural world features prominently in Thomson's work, but is central to his children's writing. Between 1966 and 1976, he published the three books in the Danny Fox series, *Danny Fox*, *Danny Fox Meets a Stranger* and *Danny Fox at the Palace*. The fox's exploits were based on folk stories, but the books also had parallels with their author's life; to start with, both he and Danny and his wife, Doxie, had three sons. The fox cubs were also three males, Lick, Chew and Swallow. In the third book, a girl cub is born, Choke. Was this the daughter that Martina and David wished for? Danny Fox was egalitarian, forgiving and humble – as well as being devoted to his family. Clíona de Bhaldraithe, whose family and the Thomson's were friends, recalls David repeatedly saying, 'I am Danny Fox'. The first book opens with the fox's mission statement:

> He used all his most cunning tricks, and was the proudest fox in the world when he came safely home from his adventures with all the food his family could want.

One of Tim Thomson's fondest memories of childhood is his father reading for him and his brothers the latest draft instalment of whichever *Danny Fox* book he was working on. 'This role for a father was supreme. We were dying for him to read it cause we know it was about us – we were the cubs, Lick, Chew and Swallow.'

Danny Fox is ingenious when fending for his family. He even uses the risky strategy of pretending to be dead, so when the fisherman throws Danny Fox's 'body' on to the cart full of fish, he 'comes alive' again and tosses fish from the cart as the fisherman drives with his back turned.

There is a social morality behind the stories, too, says Tim Thomson. The fisherman character for example: 'Danny Fox did have a conscience. And he was the underdog. But then the fisherman was a real underdog. Though the fisherman was his enemy, he embraced him. Often it was almost like living our own family through the writing.'

Regarding this relationship with his sons, in this extract from *Danny Fox Meets a Stranger*, the fox's speech is pure David Thomson:

> When there was nothing to eat, which often happened in the winter, Danny Fox used to say to his children, 'Which would you rather have – a big meal or a good story?' And usually they would answer 'A good story!' – not because they liked it better than a meal, but because he knew that they only asked that question when he had no food to give them. A story was better than nothing and if it was good, it made them forget their hunger.

Luke Thomson also remembers well the 'test readings' in Regent's Park Terrace. He's proud of the part he played in changing one detail: Danny Fox had once flown to Australia on an eagle's back. David had described the fox and eagle coming back the same route. Luke said why not have him circumnavigating the globe, to make it more interesting. David took up the suggestion. Luke has inherited his father's love for writing. A family friend, Leslie Daiken, wrote to eight-year-old Luke, describing him as 'the best writer in the Thomson family'.

In 1962, in a shaky hand from The Middlesex Hospital, David painted a scene for his son:

> My dear Luke,
>
> It is lovely when a letter comes to hospital. A man brings a bundle and puts them on a table in the middle of the ward. A nurse sorts them out and takes them round to the people in bed. One day she came to my bed and guess what she gave me? A letter from Luke! A lovely Easter card and a bright picture. Yesterday Mummy brought your doggie in a green coat. Thank you. Give her a kiss from me. Love from David.

Luke Thomson, at his home in North London.

Luke Thomson turned out to be the other writer of the family and has written three novels. Yet neither he nor his brothers are very familiar with their father's writing. It seemed to pass them by when he was alive. Perhaps they were too close to it, or their father's fiction was sometimes too close to the bone. Ben laughs recalling his father's admission in *In Camden Town* that he liked touching girls' hair on buses. The somewhat deranged character Daniel in their father's fiction caused some embarrassment. Yet they've grown to appreciate the legacy. Tim says that rereading *Nairn* recently he developed a better understanding of David. 'He had the manners of a king and the gentleness of a saint.'

All three Thomson boys were joiners or carpenters at different stages of their lives. The egalitarian in Thomson meant he didn't encourage academic achievement or the professions and had always told them to value manual work. 'All of us three boys did that and it's wonderful if you can incorporate that with a sort of intellectual life. For all the good things about him, I curse him for valuing manual work so much. We all three did it. Doing it at the time he did in Ireland in the 1930s was fine, but he was able to progress to something completely different.'

David did encourage the boys in cultural appreciation, however. In 1982 he passed on some travel advice to Luke and his French wife Irene about their planned visit to Scotland. He instructs him on visiting cousins and suggests they go to Skye and visit Sorley MacLean:

> He's a rather famous poet, writes in Gaelic and translates to English on the opposite page. Very good. Mountains beautiful and he's the best man in the world to tell you about them.
>
> In Edinburgh there's a young poet who knows us, Hayden Murphy, very keen on drinking, and if you want a guide to the most popular pubs, get him.

He concludes that they'll have a lovely time 'without any need for these people'.

Ben Thomson's abiding memory of his father is of a thoughtful, kind man. He wasn't what he calls the 'usual football dad', and completely oblivious to the fortunes of any of the London soccer teams, too. He was wrapped up in his own world. Ben remembers a man who spent a lot of time at his desk or in the pub. 'He wasn't like fathers now, who are much more involved with their children's care.' Timothy remembers a happy routine in Regent's Park Terrace. Suppertime was always 7.30 pm during his father's BBC years. His key would be heard in the door almost exactly at that time. David didn't dominate the supper conversation, according to Tim, but would listen to what the kids were saying, before he'd find a theme. 'We were always in awe of how he'd say things and how he put them together and the flow of it all. You never knew how it was going to end ... except that it would end when he reached into his jacket for the packet of Woodbine.' When he ritually struck the match, Ben and his brothers knew that was the natural end to the session.

> So Danny and Doxie and Lick and Chew and Swallow had an enormous feast. They ate and ate until they could eat no more. Then they all fell down together in a heap, fast asleep.

But Danny, in his den on the mountain, never had to deal with a family problem like his creator's. David was not Tim's biological father. In 1954 Martina had left David after meeting another man, an American intelligence officer, in Paris. They married and went to live in a village south of Naples. This was the 'shameful episode', as she referred to it in 2013. When she returned to David in 1955 she was pregnant, and Timothy was born in October that year.

When Tim was ten, his mother took him out to dinner and told him some of the story; the main news being that his father wasn't his father. 'It was an impersonal setting to be told this. She had never asked me out on my own before. According to her we were going for a treat, then she dropped this bombshell.' She told him he might find it embarrassing to tell his brothers, so she said she would but didn't, and they only found out, third-hand, years later.

Martina Thomson had a genuine dilemma. She had a ticking bomb, but sought a controlled explosion. Having made a significant mistake once in her life, she didn't want it to haunt her, but she didn't want it all out in the open either. Her solution, it seems, was to be 'economical with the truth'. David, for his part, never mentioned it to their sons. So Timothy was brought up with what he calls 'a schism that I know has affected my life. But I don't hold David responsible.'

12 Novembre, '64, Paris
Mon chere Timmy,

Il est presque huit heures du matin et j'attends Philippe O'Connor dans une café agreable qui s'appelle Le Depart.

The time is an hour different here and the street lamps have only just been switched off. A minute ago, from the pavement outside this cafe, I saw the two towers of Notre Dame in an autumn mist just as the sky was beginning to grow light. One day you will see it with me.

Martina and David's friend, Melanie Cuming, was unaware of Timothy's fatherhood issue until after Martina's death, though she always wondered why Tim didn't have David's features when Luke and Ben were so like him. Despite her closeness to Martina, she had never enquired and Martina didn't volunteer information about her ex-husband. Behind the scenes, however, she had the marriage annulled so she and David could marry, which they did in 1964 and which allowed David to adopt Tim.

Now fifty-eight, Tim has done all his investigations and that has set his mind, as he says, 'some way in peace'. Yet he describes feeling to some extent like an outsider when David was dying in 1988 because of the issue. His biological father, John Bare, worked for American military intelligence and came to the UK during World War II. He died in 1990, two years after David. Many families have 'unfinished business'. This was the Thomsons'.

The cover of the first Danny Fox *book.*

Cubs – and boys – grow up. In a scene at the start of *Danny Fox at the Palace* Danny is coming down the mountain path, sniffing the air, when he sees another fox. The other fox was growling and the hair on its back stood up on end. 'Then the other fox began to wag its tail. The hair on its back became smooth again and it walked towards Danny in a friendly way. At last Danny knew who it was. It was his own son, Swallow, who had grown up and was almost as big as him.'

All three Thomson sons had moved out of Regent's Park Terrace by the mid 1980s. Ben has lived in Brighton for many years; Timothy in Devon; Luke, after living in France, has resettled in London, off Finchley Road. As for David's adult relationship with his own father, they recall that he rarely if ever spoke about the senior Thomson. Ben says he never did, though he told him once that through a combination of pain, anger, sadness and regret, he chewed up three handkerchiefs at Alexander Thomson's funeral in 1953.

David's sister Barbara's wedding, 1948. David's parents back row, David back right (courtesy Steve Bober).

Following his mother's death two years earlier, a parishioner at her local church wrote: 'There was never the slightest condescension in her many kindly deeds. She became a real friend in the homes of those less fortunate than herself. Annie Thomson had an unfailing sense of humour. I inevitably came away from her home refreshed and made happy again by her cheerful companionship.'

Others had found qualities in her that David her son must have recognized, but had not, it appears, celebrated with his own children, for complex human reasons perhaps. Regarding David's relationship with his siblings, Martina recalled that he was never close to Mary, the eldest, or Barbara, the youngest. He got on best with Joan, who in the early 1980s helped him with research for *Nairn*.

Danny Fox's creator, shared a special affinity for the whole animal world with his mother. Hunting and shooting didn't attract him during his Woodbrook years and his memoir doesn't refer to the famous shoots on the Rockingham estate. In reviewing a biography of the great animal advocate Humanity Dick, or Richard Martin, by Shevawn Lynam in 1975, he made a reference to his own childhood:

> When I was a boy in the 1920s the instinct of my classmates was to stone a wounded bird. Most children now would nurse it back to health. This I believe is one living memorial to Richard Martin, the founder of The Society For the Prevention of Cruelty to Animals.

Thomson was a well-regarded children's writer by the 1980s. In 1985 he gave a talk to pupils in St James's Junior School in Tunbridge Wells in Kent. He recalled his childhood in Derbyshire. He described the dramatic rescue of the family dog from a swollen river by his sister, Joan, who was only nine and how he admired her always for it. She also rescued a young crow from boys who were stoning it. Their mother made a splint for the injured crow, which began stealing again, as crows do, as soon as he was well. David named him Jim Crow.

He offered the pupils advice:

> Even if you are given a subject that seems dull, and you have to do it at school for a teacher, use your imagination and always say what you really mean – not what you think other people expect you to say. It's you that matters and even the most unlikely things – button or bootlaces – become exciting if you think about them for long enough.

There is a lengthy exchange of letters with Macmillan Children's Books in 1983, David becomes uncharacteristically cranky over the delay and terms of the contract for a new series, *Flying Carpets*. Later that year he returned to his Irish contacts, looking again for inspiration for children's fiction from folklore. He was interested in stories of human babies that were allegedly suckled or brought up by animals and he wrote to Tomás de Bhaldraithe and his niece, Ríonach Uí Ógáin, now Director of the National Folklore Collection. De Bhaldraithe sent David some folk motifs that Ríonach had researched. He adds that 'the hot Paddy that you remember now costs £1.30 – but we are still at it!'

He continues: 'I've just thought of a phrase from Dineen's Dictionary that might come in useful: "Maitheas bainne cíoch an róin go ndéanaidh sé dhuit" (May it do you as much good as the seal's breast milk).' The result was *Mother Seal*, then after discussion with Gail Barron, his editor at Macmillan, *Ronan and other Stories* (1984).

David must have dreamt at least of global fame for his children's work. When Séamus Delargy wrote in 1967 congratulating him on *Danny Fox,* describing it 'as a charming book and will surely delight hosts of youngsters who must be fed up with Christopher Robin and Winnie-the-Pooh', David asked his friend to take his admiration a stage further. He wanted him to send the book to the Walt Disney Company in California, believing Delargy had an 'in', having once lunched in Burbank with its famous founder.

But already a more realisable project was on the way. David had asked Delargy's colleague, Seán O'Suilleabháin, to explain the Irish name for the town of Carrick-on-Shannon. 'Cora Druma Rúisc' means the weir at the back of the marsh, O'Suilleabháin explained, referring in his letter to 'this Roscommon project of yours'.

David was now concentrating on what became his lyrical masterpiece.

The Thomson and de Bhaldraithe families on holiday in Connemara, early 1960s (slightly out of focus). Martina is on the extreme left, David on the right, Tomás de Bhaldraithe is kneeling, his daughter Clíona is standing (Clíona de Bhaldraithe–Marsh).

10. The Memoir Triumphant

David Thomson was sitting in the lotus position on the floor of the hospital ward, his 'home from home', the Halliwick Hospital in Barnet, when a student nurse walked in on her rounds. Mary Pogue was from County Leitrim. It was the summer of 1966 and David was fifty-two years old. According to his diary, he was admitted

> After nearly four weeks of increasing mania, intense activity, and good work and high perceptive powers (or so it seems to me) and very extreme emotion, all of which reached a climax of convulsions on the night of Tuesday the 21st to 22nd of June. Martina was dealing with me with no one to help and me talking of death, which seemed to be imminent with each bout.

When Mary spoke to him, he reacted to her accent.

'Oh, an Irish colleen!', he said.

'So what might you know about Ireland?', she asked.

'Try me?', he replied.

She told him she came from Carrick-on-Shannon. He became more animated: 'Well ... there's J.P. Murray's pub ... there's Campbell's, the grocers

… and up at the corner, Flynn's?' He enquired about her name. 'Would you be any relation to a postman called George?' George Pogue, who delivered and collected mail from Woodbrook House, during Thomson's years there, was her father. This man so familiar with her part of Ireland, fascinated Mary Pogue: 'In appearance and because of the clothes he was wearing, he reminded me of Mahatma Ghandi. As I got to know him more, I found him so intelligent. Later I thought maybe even too intelligent for his own good?'

Mary Pogue discovered that the towns and landscape of Leitrim and Roscommon were vivid in his memory. It was a recollection that was germinating and would find expression soon in the writing of his memoir, *Woodbrook*.

Following David Thomson's death in 1988, Mary Pogue's neighbour, John McGahern, described *Woodbrook* as: 'One of those books that abolishes time and establishes memory. I think of it as an Indian summer in our literature that will never fade. The literary quality of this book is strange and mysterious and completely individual.'* In *Woodbrook*, the reader is brought on an evocative journey, where the well near the house is described as much more than merely a source of fresh water: 'The heart of Woodbrook was a natural spring called by some the spring well or the boiling well and by those who used its water daily as the Well. It boiled very cold and seemed to me holy and secret long before I thought about the meaning of the Holy Wells of Ireland.'

Woodbrook has many such simple observations – of people, places, and country tasks. When Winnie Mulvey, the cook and housekeeper, decides to leave her job at the house, David writes how they were never close emotionally, but nonetheless had a bond, made over many cups of tea standing at the range in 'her' kitchen. There's a sense here of the chemistry of friendship and even a hint of flirtatiousness, in a celebration of how ordinary tasks can become profound, reminiscent of the observations of Kavanagh or Heaney:

> On her butter-making days I never passed the dairy without going in to take a turn on the churn. Nor did any other man of course; it would be unfriendly and unlucky not to. Sometimes I kept on churning long after she wished to resume it because I loved the moment when the butter came, the change in rhythm, the thud, thud, thud of solid lumps created in the liquid. And to watch her washing new butter was beautiful – in the water I had drawn from the boiling well.

---

* John McGahern speaking at the David Thomson memorial evening, Royal Irish Academy, Dublin, February 1989.

The view from Woodbrook House, looking north to Lough Edin, known locally as Drumharlow Lake.

But when David returned to Woodbrook many years later in June 1968, he found Winnie's churn lying broken and abandoned outside the stable yard.

Woodbrook is rich in impressionistic incident. When he and Phoebe are in a boat on Drumharlow Lake, so intoxicated are they with their own company that a grove of trees turns out to be a mirage. He relates a darker incident, when the younger Kirkwood, Tony, discovers a human skull and brings it back to the house. In showing Ivy's horrified reaction, David alludes to a fear of bad karma for the family that might result from this piece of childish innocence, as if some kind of dark forces had been stirred.

Thomson's belief in the importance of knowledge and regard for the past, a theme in *Nairn in Darkness and Light*, returns here: When Phoebe at twelve years old has just recovered from a serious illness, he thinks that she must now understand the symbolism of St Lassair's Well, the healing well in nearby Ballyfarnon.

And what of the critical reaction to *Woodbrook?* Martina Thomson recalled that sales of the book accelerated following Bill Webb's review in *The Guardian*: 'Half way through I knew that this was one of those books which would leave marks in the memory like the scars of personal experience.' Webb didn't see the David and Phoebe relationship as the 'innocent love affair' it has sometimes been described as. Yet his bluntness risks missing the book's subtlety: 'He followed her, burning, everywhere – on horseback, in the field, lying awake in the room next to hers, sharing the same chair for Latin lessons in an innocent erotic haze of all-but lovemaking which must have fairly lit up the sexually murky Irish countryside for miles around.'

Jennifer Johnston's review was tenderer: 'Some people are worshippers, others critics, and most of the rest of us are merely day-to-day accepters and forgetters. Mr Thomson is a worshipper. His book is a hymn to a child-girl, a family and a corner of Ireland and a way of life, then disintegrating in front of his eyes, now well gone.'

On the RTÉ programme, 'Imprint', in May 1975, Seamus Heaney, once more got the measure of Thomson's writing: 'Being in love of course is an intensely enlivening experience, especially if you're eighteen and in a new and beautiful countryside. The whole nervous system tingles afresh, experience is surcharged with delight, the proximity of the loved one makes everything within range precious.'

Heaney wrote to David that his 'delight in the book was that special kind which I call "the jealousy test" – I am jealous that somebody else had written it – and it enlivened all kinds of memories and impulses in me.' He recommends John McGahern's work to David and says when he's in that part of the country next time, he will 'spy on Woodbrook'.

Woodbrook was republished in several editions and found many new and loyal friends over the years. One is the BBC foreign correspondent, Fergal Keane. In his introduction to the Folio edition in 2007, he says it's a book he returns to again and again:

> If you have never visited the wild landscapes of Counties Sligo, Leitrim and Roscommon, David Thomson's evocation of lakes and mountains will surely draw you there. I often carry the book with me on my journeys far afield. I do so precisely because of Thomson's ability to take me back to the beauty of green drumlins and leaden skies reflected in lake water. With *Woodbrook* I can smell the damp hills, even in the Iraqi desert.

Praise for the work didn't just come from the famous or literary professionals. Eugene Judge from Kiltimagh, County Mayo, was one of the many ordinary readers who wrote to David: 'My wife told me I've talked of nothing else for ten days!' Erika Casey, a German-born woman living in Salthill, Galway, was so taken with the book that she decided to translate it into German. When David discovered this he wrote to Barrie & Rockliff requesting leniency in regard to rights with the publisher she had found, as he said, 'she did it for the love of it'. Benzinger published the translation in 1985.

A letter came from David's old flame, Rita Kiernan Biddulph, in December 1974:

> The love story was beautifully written and made me cry. Then I laughed out loud at the account of that lorry journey. It's a sad book too and very lonely, I suppose growing up is – it is for me.
>
> Best wishes for '75 to you and yours.
>
> Love,
>
> Rita

The BBC Radio 4 programme 'Kaleidoscope' had a discussion in December 1974 between the presenter, Paul Vaughan, and the writer Maeve Binchy. She was very taken with the book, Vaughan less so. He was disappointed with 'the way in which you never knew which way he [Thomson] was moving'. Binchy, by contrast, said that this was a great relief to her:

> I studied history and I'm sick and tired of people who are always so predictable in the way they were moving about through history ... either you were for the Irish, good or bad, or you were for England or British settlers the whole way and they could do no wrong. He seems to be a man who wrote without censure ... his only bitterness is against senseless violence whichever side it was committed by.

Perhaps, as all great writing, readers see different observations in various passages. For Seamus Heaney on 'Imprint' it was the way Thomson observed Charlie Kirkwood's insomnia. For John McGahern, speaking in 1989, it was a passage about bees and their behaviour, in this case with keepers who were his friends, the colourful Moroney brothers. Tim Dee, then, asserts that Thomson is engaged in 'a sensual seeking at the same time as an intellectual one', and finds symbolism in a passage where David out horse-riding replaces a branch filling a gap in a hedge, seeing it as a metaphorical leaving of one world, the natural world, for another, the human environment.

Woodbrook's publication wasn't short on the comment and analysis that generates sales: how accurate or how balanced was the history ... how credible was the love story? Cathal O'Shannon hosted a discussion on RTÉ television in January 1975 when his guests were Michael O'Callaghan, editor of the *Roscommon Herald* and Joanne Clements, who had lived near Woodbrook in another Anglo-Irish Big House, Lough Rynn Castle, near Mohill. O'Callaghan described it as a 'remarkable book'. Clements didn't care for the love story. 'I think it's a kind of old man's fancy. It sounds horrible and I should be ashamed of myself, but I think he's blown this up over the years.' She added, unsympathetically: 'When she [Ivy Kirkwood] knew he had a fixation on the child, why did she keep him?' The actor and writer Jeananne Crowley had a completely different female perspective describing it in *The Irish Times* in 1977 as 'the best book on love written by a man' and 'the most evocative writing on first love I have ever read'.

David now engaged somewhat reluctantly in the 'housekeeping' of being a writer. His papers contain a considerable number of letters concerning the distribution of *Woodbrook*. He did his own survey towards the end of 1974 and listed the bookshops that were either out of stock or hadn't taken the book at all. He wrote to Barrie and Jenkins (by then part of Hutchinson) and got a reply from John Pattison on 29 November, who said, 'We are not quite as incompetent or casual about them as you seem to think.' David had also asked why it hadn't been advertised up till then. Pattison explains that they were waiting for reviews to quote, but that they would now go ahead. It's clear from further letters that David had got quite angry at the publishers, for one thing because of the many copies that were misbound, with sections out of sequence. Séamus Delargy's copy was one of these. Cathal O'Shannon of RTÉ could only find a flawed copy when he went to Fred Hanna's Bookshop in Dublin. David then expresses disappointed that the publishers can't understand his frustration. He at one stage apologized for the 'angry way I expressed myself' at a meeting with the publishers. He also complained that *Woodbrook* wasn't in a local Camden bookshop, but books by Claire Tomalin and Beryl Bainbridge were.

And what of the David's health in the Woodbrook years? *Woodbrook's* pages only obliquely refer to it. But Percy Carty, now in his late eighties, is one of the very few local people who remember Woodbrook in the late 1930s, recalls an incident that coloured his view of David. Carty held the keys to the tower of Cloontykilla Castle on the nearby Rockingham estate. One day David decided he wanted to climb it but Percy refused him the keys, saying his employer, Cecil King-Harmon, didn't allow it. According to Percy, David grabbed the keys, entered the tower, locked it from the inside and spent several hours there. Carty describes it as an act of arrogance, which he didn't like, though he is a great admirer of *Woodbrook*. In hindsight, it might be explained more easily as the action of a person seeking solitude. In his diary of 7 August 1945, the day after the Hiroshima bomb, David recalls 'Phoebe's irritation at me, in my old state of neurotic depression.' He's also reminded in the diary of what he calls his 'faith at Woodbrook',

> A faith in natural growth. On one occasion I was drawing timber in a heavy frost. I was in a fit of black gloom, but the faith was strong and cheered me when I thought that whatever destruction men do amongst themselves, the trees and grass and all the rest live on. Faith gave me the only tangible consolation when I read the bad news yesterday about atomic energy.

There's a passage in *Woodbrook* that reveals David's mental equilibrium in the early 1940s. The night after Phoebe leaves the house for good, David, driven by melancholy and loneliness, burnt the notebooks he had accumulated throughout his years there, one by one in the middle of the night, after reviving the dying embers of the kitchen fire.

> I think it was the most destructive thing I have ever done. I think it was mad. And whatever the unconscious motive – purification by fire, killing that part of my spirit to let it be re-born, burning the tangible signs of my past to set my imagination free – the outcome was the opposite. It brought me no relief; it aggravated that tortuous searching state of mind; the next day I had an awful sense of loss.

Not dissimilar doubts returned many years later as he worked on the book. Though *Woodbrook* became regarded as a 'minor classic', David blew hot and cold about it. He had a draft of about a third of the book written when he told Martina that he thought it wasn't working. He asked for her opinion, as he always did. She read it, was enthralled, and told him it was wonderful. David was so disappointed in his efforts that he had tried to find money to pay back the advance from the publishers. Then he decided to carry on. 'I think I convinced him,' she said.

His doubts may have also come from discussion with the publishers about the shape of the book and its very wide canvas. An editor at Barrie & Jenkins, Matthew Evans, wrote the report on receiving the first 35,000 words, saying it wasn't an easy book to follow. 'It starts off with his arrival at Woodbrook, a meal, conversation, horses, then it takes off all over the place.' He comments on the Kirkwood family quite sarcastically: 'Although now in decline, all the family were still totally horse obsessed and spent most of its time on the back of one animal or another.'

Although he thinks it being 'bitty', and that it demands concentration, it's also clear that he believed Thomson was on to something. So Barrie & Jenkins went ahead.

David had begun work on *Woodbrook* during the 1960s. His notebooks record research visits to Roscommon and Leitrim; a diary entry for Tuesday, 5 August 1968, notes that the Carrick-on-Shannon Regatta had been held the preceding weekend. Shane Flynn drove the family to Woodbrook, where they had tea in the old servants' hall. They rowed on Lough Key in search of pike. They looked for a particular inlet where apparently the fishing was good, but, on Flynn's advice, the Thomsons didn't venture far because they were only in a small punt and the lake could be treacherous. When they did get to fish, Tim Thomson recalls one detail from that summer: you only had to put a spinner in the water and you'd be landing huge pike. Tim had been used to very meagre catches from the canal in Camden Town: 'I remember thinking, "Yes, there really are big fish and you can actually catch them." '

David describes encountering brambles and overgrowth everywhere that summer, at Woodbrook and at the Rockingham estate. He also refers to the dispute at that time over the title of the castle at Rockingham, between The King-Harmons and McDermotts, a sombre postscript to the story of the once mighty Anglo-Irish families of this area. The McDermott's ruled this area until it was granted to the King family from England under the Cromwellian settlement, during the 1660s.

There's also a connection between Rockingham and the north London district where David lived for most of his life. The famous architect John Nash, who designed Rockingham House in 1809, had also designed Regent's Park and Regent's Street.

David recounts how he was immediately recognized by a local man, John Lowe, in the famous Henry's in Cootehall. 'He was only ten years old when he last saw me in his father's shop. When people recognize me and talk about the old days reminding me of what I did, I remember but feel as though we are speaking of someone else – a person whom I and they used to know long ago.'

Woodbrook House today.

Tommy Maxwell, who was then a joint owner of Woodbrook with his brother, Jimmy, wrote to David after the family had returned to London. He had really enjoyed the talk and the drinking they'd done together, it reminded him of the old times. 'What do your boys think of us Irish guys? I'm sure they are saying, we are quare fellows.'

Continuing his research a year later in October 1969, David contacted Cecil King-Harmon, then living in St Catherine's Park, Leixlip, making a nostalgic connection. The elderly man says that, after the 1957 fire, he thought of rebuilding Rockingham House on Nash's original plans, this time as a two-storey house, but it would have cost £150,000, so wasn't possible. He said he and his wife decided to 'sell out lock, stock and barrel to the Land Commission' and concludes stoically that this present address is 'more suitable under present conditions'.

There is another 'footnote' to the King-Harmon story in Thomson's papers, a letter from Séamus Kelly, formerly drama critic and then columnist with *The Irish Times*, congratulating David on *Woodbrook* and telling a story about the King-Harmons. Friends of Kelly's had taken a boat on Lough Key just after the war, one of them being Seán McBride, the former IRA leader who went on to become a government minister in 1948 and a Nobel Laureate in 1974. When they anchored off Rockingham, a ghillie arrived by boat to ask them to move on, that they were obstructing the squire's view. As an indication, perhaps, of the changed nature of power in Ireland, they defied the request, stayed put and received no further interference.

Woodbrook never made the bestsellers list but remains in print forty years after it was first published. Its admirers are many. The book's virtues are also its liabilities to some extent: when the love story is in full flow, it's a 'page turner', but when Thomson gets scholarly, whether about the Great Famine or the events of 1798, concentration is required. Thomson was true to his own vision, but he left many readers perhaps wondering exactly what kind of a book were they dealing with.

Of all *Woodbrook*'s achievements, the most enduring is its creation of an abiding mystery and fascination with its central female character, Phoebe Kirkwood.

The Woodbrook lands today, with the house behind trees. The marshy area in the foreground was known as "the bottoms" and referred to several times by David Thomson as a special place.

11. Phoebe

David Thomson put such power into *Woodbrook's* love story that Phoebe Kirkwood has become legendary, even luminescent. We know she was talented, classically beautiful, mysterious and remembered by many *Woodbrook* devotees as something of an idyllic example of womanhood. She could equally be described simply as a privileged young woman who died young.

During times when David was in London and she in Roscommon, Phoebe wrote in detail to him with all the local news, including events like ceremonies in Ardcarne Church. On one occasion his sister Barbara, who was staying with the Kirkwood's, caused a stir after getting a fit of the giggles during a service.

Phoebe was conscious of her class, too. In one letter she describes how Winnie Mulvey, the cook at Woodbrook, was disappointed that David wasn't coming over from London as expected, gently mocking the local woman's use of English with quotation marks, saying Winnie was 'horrid disappointed'.

She writes of horses, their exploits and even their personalities, humanizing them with their names. In another letter she asks him to buy her a pair of Marks & Spencer trousers, specifying the size; waist 28–30, 'with the longest legs you can find'. David had access to the Kirkwood house in St John's Wood and was often asked to go there if the Kirkwood's were in Roscommon, to supervise decoration or rearrangements of furniture.

At the end of 1944, following his last visit to Dublin and the passionate kiss described towards the end of the book, Phoebe addresses David as 'my dear'. If there was any doubt that their feelings were mutual, this letter is proof: 'I think I bore up remarkably well after your departure – don't you? A very few tears the night before and an untroubled sleep on the fatal morning. I wonder when you'll be back – it feels all wrong not to be able to see you.'

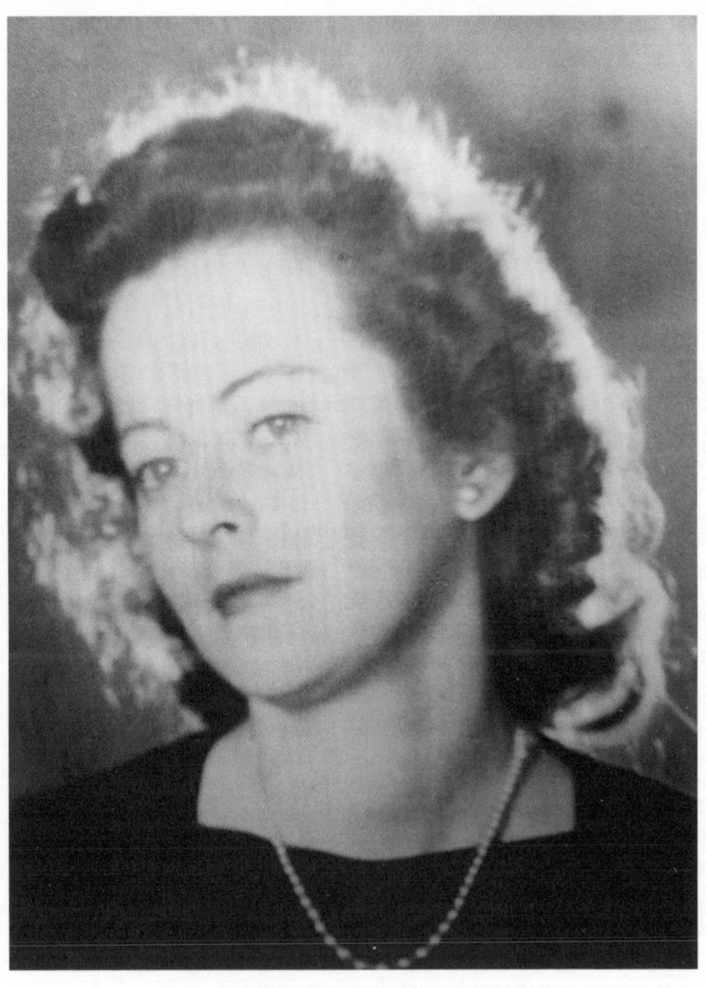

A photograph of Phoebe Kirkwood, probably taken in the early 1940s (courtesy Lionel Gallagher).

She shows a sense of more global matters, too. In a letter in 1943 she writes about a young man staying with her family in Sutton House. He was a French government minister's son, but it is the Vichy government. He's a pleasant boy, she relates, but she has reservations: 'One can't help feeling rather bitter about anyone representing Vichy.' She recounts to him a night where her parents stayed up very late to hear Prime Minister Chamberlain addressing the British people after the Munich Conference in September 1938. They had been to a thanksgiving service in Ardcarne Church that evening. It was a gloomy time: 'Mummy and I just wanted to sing ourselves hoarse, but when we got there it was all uninspiring with three hapless parsons and the gloomiest sermon you've ever heard. All about how we probably wouldn't see another harvest.'

She ends this very long letter with:

> I've just read 'La Belle Dame'. The woman with six children under 4 must have been pretty busy?
>
> Love from Phoebe
>
> Some letter, isn't it?

She was annoyed on hearing of nurses from the Knockvicar area leaving their hospital posts in London when war was in prospect without giving notice, saying: 'Don't you call that really despicable … hospital nurses!!!'

As well as her own father's military background, she would probably have been thinking of the King-Harmons, whose only son, Thomas was serving in the British army and later killed in action.

Rev James McCormick, the rector at Arcarne's daughter Deirdre, volunteered for the services in England and was assigned to drive ambulances. Her son, Christopher Ashe, an art-gallery owner in Dublin, recalls a story his mother used to tell. She had arrived at Boyle railway station on leave one time when she noticed Thomas King-Harmon on the other platform waiting for the Dublin train on his way to the Front. They waved. It was the last time she saw him.

Had Phoebe other admirers? In a letter from Kilmacanogue sometime in 1943 she mentions a young Australian who had been staying there, and a long letter he wrote saying nice things about her, that she was, as she quotes him, 'lovely + vital, etc., etc.', before adding a note of reassuring detachment: 'One always seems to impress the people one isn't interested in, doesn't one?'

At this time, the renowned artist Paul Henry, who had lived on Achill for many years, moved to the townland called Carrigoona, near Glencot, where the Kirkwoods were living. Phoebe writes about Mabel Young, Henry's student who became his second wife. A local woman had described her as, 'very good at painting the butts of beech trees coming out of moss', and the young Kirkwood thought it a 'sweet description of someone's work'. Her informant, referred to as Kitty, suggests it would be better to say that she specializes in trees. Phoebe then points out that there weren't many beech trees 'up there', so she was told that Mabel Young 'did them from memory'.

In another long letter to David on 31 December 1944 she mentions that she likes the doctor who is attending her, Dr McDonald, who she'd seen again that day because her temperature was still high. She couldn't think of anything to say to him so she told him about a dream she'd had the night before, in which she'd given birth to numerous children – including twins – in the Woodbrook hayshed. She wonders what the doctor might think, then observes:

> I've just thought that if he's anything like you he'll put some kind of horrid Freudian meaning to that ... Don't suppose you can read this, but I'm feeling much better tempered now so I'll stop.
>
> Love
>
> Phoebe

Early in 1945, Phoebe became seriously ill with what was later diagnosed as miliary or disseminated tuberculosis, a chronic form of TB, that spreads rapidly from the lungs to other organs. She was a patient in the Merrion Nursing Home in Herbert Street, Dublin. As Phoebe's health deteriorated, Ivy Kirkwood wrote to David:

> It would only be dreadful for you to come here, though selfishly I wish you could – it's the silence I find so truly awful – you know how inarticulate most people are – I haven't talked to Tony because she gets so shattered. When anything happened to any of us, Phoebe and I were so in the habit of looking at it together, to suddenly find myself so completely alone is beyond anything one can realise in a day, in a week, it is like a mountain of blackness coming nearer and nearer ...

On 18 January, still in the Merrion Nursing Home and very ill at this stage, Phoebe writes: 'I had the hairdresser to do my hair today – what luxury?' In a long letter to David a month after Phoebe's death, Ivy recalls her daughter's last hours:

I seemed to be having a perfectly normal conversation with Phoebe inside my head, and we talked about many things and finally came to the business of her illness and what to do about it, and she said she hated her body and didn't want to have to bother about it anymore. She asked me if it was very difficult to get free of it.

This letter is long, yet Ivy doesn't seem to be able to bring herself to mention the moment of her daughter's death. A Canon Grey came to the home for the anointing: 'As soon as she heard the words of The Lord's Prayer, she began saying them ...' Ivy describes how the whole situation got too much for her. In her distress and confusion, she wanted the clergyman gone. Then she and Phoebe were alone for the last time:

– I feel so lost, when shall we get together again?
– In the morning, I said.
She quite contentedly settled down to sleep.
–Oh good.

She died on 9 February 1945. Her funeral took place in Enniskerry, County Wicklow. James McCormick, formerly of Ardcarne, officiated. Phoebe's resting place is in the cemetery of St Patrick's overlooking the village.

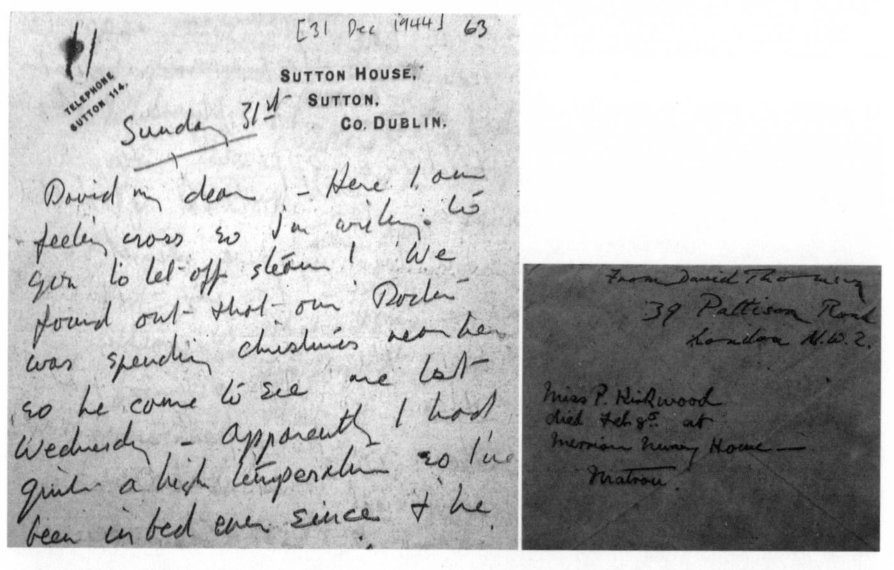

[31 Dec 1944] 63

Telephone Sutton 114.

Sutton House,
Sutton,
Co. Dublin.

Sunday 31st

David my dear – Here I am feeling cross so I'm writing to you to let off steam! We found out that our Doctor was spending Christmas near here so he came to see me last Wednesday – apparently I had quite a high temperature so I've been in bed ever since & he

From David [illegible]
39 Pattison Road
London N.W.2.

Miss P. Kirkwood
died Feb 8th at
Merrion Nursing Home —
Matron

Left: *One of the last letters Phoebe Kirkwood wrote to David, December 31, 1944, in which she mentions having a temperature.* Right: *The envelope of a letter addressed to Phoebe at the Merrion Nursing Home, Dublin, in David's handwriting, and posted in 7 February 1945, two days before she died.It was returned by the matron.*

An appreciation appeared in *The Irish Times* on 15 February 1945:

The death last week of Phoebe Kirkwood came as a sad shock to many. In her short life of 22 years, she threw happiness into all she did, whether it was farming at home, making a frock for her first ball, playing the violin with exceeding skill, acting or painting pictures. After her recent exhibitions, artists had predicted a rosy future for her. She was like a spring flower and her fragrance will remain a beautiful memory to all who mourn her.

[Page 11]

BURIALS in Powerscourt Parish in the Diocese of Glendalough in the year 1945

Name.	Abode.	When Buried.	Age.	By whom the Ceremony was performed.
Phoebe Kirkwood No. 69	Glenart	Feby 10 1945	23	F. MacCormick M.B.A. Byrne
Aileen D. F. James	Hampstead Mental Home Glasnevin	March 26 1945	78	M.B.A. Byrne

Phoebe Kirkwood's burial record at Saint Patrick's Church, Enniskerry.

Phoebe Kirkwood's grave in St Patrick's Cemetery Enniskerry, County Wicklow.

But any look at David Thomson's life must raise several questions about the chronology of the relationship and the presence of other women in his life, how much of the Phoebe story is real and how much is 'literary'. First, David was engaged to Jacqueline Wynmalen in 1934, only two years after the start of his strong feelings for the young Kirkwood, according to his account in the book. This is not inconsistent, however. We could assume that feelings for Phoebe burned brighter in the latter years of the 1930s, when the relationship with Jacqueline had ended and Phoebe was sixteen or older.

Martina Thomson suspected that the Wynmalen rejection was very hurtful for David because, although he was such an open person, he never talked about it. We know from his letters how deeply and passionately he felt for different women in his life. So was it his imagination or his recollection that made Phoebe his great love? In the 1986 RTÉ radio documentary, 'The Story of Woodbrook', he referred to what he called 'faction' in his work, a combination of fact and fiction. 'I find it difficult to draw the distinction between fact and fiction in my writing, because I can't write anything without a certain amount of fiction-sounding stuff ... in the same way that people's dreams often become a part of real life afterwards.'

Then there's Rita Kiernan. In a diary entry from January 1946 he notes that 1945 was the year that began with Phoebe's death and ended with his meeting Rita. There's also the strong letter evidence. In one to David in early 1945, Ivy Kirkwood mentions that since Phoebe was at that stage too unwell to read David's letters to her, Ivy took the liberty of destroying them, which suggests an emotional intimacy between the couple that she didn't want to intrude upon.

Woodbrook readers might wonder how a person married to David Thomson might have felt about this 'other woman'. Martina Thomson said she was jealous of other women in David's life, but never of Phoebe, whom she described as a 'holy character'. David was always utterly taken by Phoebe, Martina recalled in her eighty-ninth year. Martina recalled also the book's closing section, where David speculates as to whether he could renew the relationship at that point, the moment after their passionate kiss on Howth Head at the end of 1944.

The notion of 'what might have been' naturally adds to the story's appeal. We know from the warmth of the early-1940s letters from Phoebe to David and from Ivy Kirkwood's remarks in her own letters, that David had a special bond with her elder daughter. The fact that there was no sexual intercourse involved only adds to its potency. Whether, in the end, it was love recollected or love embellished by the writer then in his late fifties, it doesn't really take from its power as a story. When he loved someone, as Martina would testify, he didn't do it by halves. And he knew how to express love.

So the Phoebe legend lives on. One of her paintings hangs in Strokestown House, County Roscommon, and has a fascination for many admirers of the book, regardless of its artistic merits. It's a representation of two Woodbrook horses drawing a plough under ominous skies. Phoebe had written once to David in London about this same painting, referring to it as 'them' rather than 'it', revealing, perhaps, the importance of horses in the Kirkwood world:

> Dear David,
>
> I've sold a picture!!!!!! Xx
>
> My horses for 3 guineas! Olive Packenham-Mahon has bought them. She told Mummy she wanted to buy them when she came to the meet here on Thursday. Isn't it most wonderfully nice of her? I'm going to take the whole family out when we get to London. …

Phoebe's painting of the two Woodbrook horses, Carnaby and Jim (courtesy Strokestown Park).

Are there any people still alive with memories of her? Bridget Timothy, now in her eighty-fifth year and living in Surrey, knew Phoebe when her family lived in Sutton House in the mid 1940s. Bridget's mother was Violet Jameson, a sister-in-law of Billy Kirkwood, Charlie's brother. She remembers Phoebe as, 'a most lovely girl, a great sharer of life with others'. Older than her and someone she looked up to, Phoebe introduced her to what was then a wartime trend of using hairnets, or snoods, partly as a 'girly' fashion statement, but also to show commitment to the war effort.

In 1988 Martina Thomson discovered several poems among David's papers written in Woodbrook during 1942. One was about Phoebe:

She came young out of shadowed places lightly,
In the rain walking,
And had driven tilted carts in blue and crimson,
Over hammocks tossed,
Swinging, rolling where winter trees are,
Herself alone driven,
Out of shadowed places,
In the rain.

In 2013 Judy Cameron, the archivist at Saint Patrick's Church, Enniskerry, County Wicklow, identified plot O 69 as Phoebe Kirkwood's unmarked grave. It remains a mystery as to why there was no headstone erected in the years following her death. The Kirkwoods had returned to live in London but this doesn't explain the omission, given the tragedy the family had endured.

12. The Woodbrook Legacy

John McGahern's comment in 1989 that *Woodbrook*, 'abolishes time and establishes memory' was echoed by what David Thomson himself said, less than a year before his death when he made his last return visit to Woodbrook, to be interviewed by Joe Mulholland of RTÉ: 'Good times are always mixed with bad times in most peoples' lives. You don't have purely good times. You have love, you have quarrels, and you have difficulties. But it all distils in a man or woman's memory; it distils itself somehow into pleasurable memories. And nostalgia is a mixture of some sort of pleasure, and a lot of pain, isn't it?'

Charles and Ivy Kirkwood didn't succeed in selling Woodbrook until after the war ended. They were living again in Kilmacanogue, County Wicklow, on the Jameson estate, when Ivy wrote to David, sometime in 1945: 'This is a very short letter to tell you that there was no bid at the auction yesterday. It was awful, not a single murmur from anybody. It was all over in 5 minutes. So we just came out.'

Despite their outward affection for the Kirkwoods over the years, the Maxwell brothers had organized a local boycott of the auction, in the hope of buying it, eventually. The tension caused by friendship, loyalty and Thomson's sense of justice all competing is one part of the book's features, because David was very friendly with the brothers, particularly Tommy. Lionel Gallagher, from Carrick, a teenager at the time, recalls seeing the slogan painted on the bridge in the town – 'Boycott the sale of Woodbrook'. Around that same time, he remembers seeing David Thomson and Charlie Kirkwood in the back room of Lowe's bar, presumably discussing their predicament.

In a remark by Ivy in an undated letter to David, probably later in 1945, an old familiar *Woodbrook* theme returns: 'Bobo [Charlie Kirkwood's nickname] is much occupied with the debates about the Republic, he is taking it all very much to heart, quite surprising as he has listened to Radio Éireann before!' What she presumably meant was that nationalist sentiments on the radio station should not have surprised him.

The family settled again in London, in Halsey Street, Knightsbridge, where Charlie predeceased his wife in 1966. Ivy died in January 1983. Antoinette (also known as Tony), Phoebe's younger sister who also features in *Woodbrook*, studied at the Royal Irish Academy of Music and became a well-known composer of ballet music, as well as songs, sonatas and one symphony. She also accompanied her mother, who in her later life resumed her career as a performer of lieder, the art songs associated with Schubert and Mahler.

David had renewed his friendship with Ivy Kirkwood in 1966, and visited her regularly in Halsey Street while writing *Woodbrook*. Antoinette, who had married a writer, Richard Phibbs, in 1961, was also a frequent visitor.

Martina Thomson recalled Antoinette's opposition to the book both preceding and following its publication. This contrasts with her joyful letters to David, now among his papers, written when she was a child, full of drawings of horses and signed 'Love, Tony'. Antoinette later tried to have the plans for a BBC radio dramatization stopped. According to Martina, David's depiction of his relationship with her elder sister, when barely a teenager, was what upset her most.

Antoinette Kirkwood died in January 2014 in a London nursing home. Her daughter, Jessica Phibbs, continues to express the family's unease with David's book and has issues with how the Kirkwood family was portrayed, but is unwilling to elaborate. Thomson had revealed certain things about the family and had refrained from mentioning others. He describes a moment when Charlie Kirkwood became somewhat intimate with a young female houseguest of David's age. However, according to Martina Thomson, he chose not to reveal that Antoinette's father wasn't Major Kirkwood, but a houseguest with whom Ivy Kirkwood had once had an affair.

David Thomson's papers, all of which are in the National Library of Scotland in Edinburgh, contain an amount of additional material that never made it to the finished memoir. There's a reflection on Andy Moroney, who featured in the book's bee episode. This was a local family who gave the young John McGahern access to their modest library. Andy Moroney, like David, suffered from illness as a child, and was sheltered by his mother. David concludes:

> He was therefore lonely and eccentric as a young man – or perhaps that is to simplify too much the reason for his loneliness. Other men have grown up lonely in large happy families. But he was protected by his mother from experience of life outside his house and when she died was brutally exposed – as too-hygienically reared babies are exposed to infection in America.

After the publication of *Woodbrook*, he found himself in a small controversy about his assertion that a practice had once existed in Ireland called *ius primae noctis*, or *droit de signeur*, where the lord or landowner allegedly insisted on sexual relations with their tenants' daughters before their wedding day. David took the doubting of this oral history very seriously and re-quotes his sources in letters on the subject. The first source was a reference to leases granted by the Earl of Cavan in the eighteenth century asserting this 'right'. Thomson refers to letters quoted by Edward MacLysaght in *Irish Life in the Seventeenth Century* (1969). His other source was local; Willie Maxwell told him of the fate of one woman at the hands a landlord in the area, Charles Coote. When she refused his advances, she was cruelly killed – or so the story went.

The issue raises an undercurrent in the locality, too. Christopher Ashe recalls that his mother, Deirdre McCormick, was of the view that David Thomson believed too much of what the Maxwell brothers told him. Also, according to local sources, the Maxwell family had been involved in the IRA during the War of Independence, which wouldn't have endeared them to those of the McCormick's tradition. 'He spent too much time listening to that stuff', was how she put it, Ashe recalls.

In his study published in *Béaloideas* in 1988, Séamas Mac Philib, makes the point that those accused of the practice in folk tradition weren't just the

Anglo-Irish gentry, but Gaelic chiefs, like the O'Flahertys of County Galway. In his conclusion he says:

> It has been noted that the Irish folk tradition of *ius primae noctis* is not borne out by other types of sources to any significant extent, but that there is a much greater degree of concurrence between folk tradition and other types of sources with regard to other forms of sexual behavior of the landed classes.*

Ríonach Uí Ógáin, Director of the National Folklore Collection at UCD concludes: 'It would be against both Common Law and Canon Law and, most likely, the various forms of Early Irish Law too. It appears in literature, as a nifty plot device. Put another way, had it existed, we'd have accounts of its suppression or campaigns for its suppression just as we do for concubinage from various different periods in Irish history.'

Thomson's *Woodbrook* research notebooks record Ivy Kirkwood's reaction to Cecil King-Harmon's view that the Allies should go to war with Russia after the Second World War ended. She had a 'feeling of despair – one terrible war to end and another to begin'. She remembered too, the English involvement in the war against the Bolsheviks after the First World War.

On 13 November 1983 the radio dramatization of *Woodbrook* by Philip Donnellan, produced by Maurice Leitch, was broadcast on BBC Radio 3. It starred Sian Phillips as Ivy, Janina Faye as Phoebe and Maurice Denham as David.

One of the techniques used is a voice – David's – asking Phoebe questions:

> (English newsreader announcing the invasion by Mussolini of Abyssinia 1935)
> Was that the year we first drifted down the river to Cootehall?
> Which was the year I waited outside the Prince Albert [Hospital in London] for the doctor to go?
> (Train screams)
> Oh God, I knew she'd die … I knew she'd die …

In another section towards the end, another ethereal voice is used, counterpointed to the passage describing Phoebe's departure in the snow: 'VOICE: *Woodbrook belongs to us*'. David then gets up in the middle of the night to burn his notebooks, the voice returns: 'VOICE: (insistent) *Woodbrook belongs to us.*'

* Séamas Mac Philib in *Béaloideas* (An Cumann Le Béaloideas Éireann/The Folklore of Ireland Society, 1988).

David had written to Donnellan in November 1977, complimenting him on the script and saying, modestly, that 'he had succeeded in making drama where essentially nothing much happens'. He goes on to discuss with Donnellan the difficulty of representing Ivy Kirkwood in the drama, as she was still alive. The BBC had a rule about representing living people without their consent. This is an indication that not only Tony, but also Ivy Kirkwood was unhappy with the book, contrary to Martina Thomson's recollections in 2013. David tells Donnellan in the letter that Ivy was 'very distressed by the book' and that Tony had kept 'a hostile silence' since its publication. In the end the drama was not broadcast until after Ivy's death in 1983.

The lack of 'action' in the *Woodbrook* story was an issue in several unsuccessful attempts over the years to develop a film version, at one stage involving the Irish director, Thaddeus O'Sullivan, with a production company, Little Bird, for RTÉ. However, the project didn't get beyond a screenplay. Jennifer Johnston had been commissioned to write the script. She says now that it wasn't very good, as despite considerable success as a novelist, she had never attempted a screenplay before. She didn't get to grips with its lyrical side and included too much dialogue, she reflects. 'Like so many other examples, it's probably best left as a book.' Thomson's art would be hard for filmmakers to capture, she believes, though 'The French, on the other hand, do this kind of thing beautifully.'

There are several letters in The National Library of Scotland between David and the playwright Brian Friel, who had an option on the film rights for a period in 1977. Friel talks about its 'lyrical flow, understatement, affection, underlying Chekovian sadness – these I think would be lost in TV'. He thought it needed a large cinematic treatment.

The actor Cyril Cusack addressed the subject in a letter to David in November 1985. They had been friends since the 1950s. 'Often and often I speak of you – and *Woodbrook*, a classic; often and often I say how filmical it is, visibly and atmospherically.'

One *Woodbrook* film script did emerge in 1987, which so alarmed David that, using whatever rights he retained, he stopped it going into production. It was easy to see why; the story had David and Phoebe in bed close to the start, as well as somewhat overegged scenes where horses were mutilated in the dead of night by dark forces as a way of terrorizing the gentry.

Carrick-on-Shannon today.

A postscript to *Woodbrook*'s publication is contained in a letter David Thomson wrote to Tennyson Hallam, assistant head of BBC Radio Drama in September 1974. He suggested that the Carrick-on-Shannon workhouse would be a suitable subject for a feature programme on Radio 3, as well as the French landing at Killala in 1798. Hallam replies stating his view that a lot had been done already on the Irish famine period. Then, turning to the 1798 suggestion, which he thinks is 'too marginal an event', he concludes revealingly: 'Might it make an interesting comedy, if you ever thought of turning your hand to playwriting?'

And what of the people associated with the book? Winnie Mulvey the cook, who left Woodbrook when she married, settled in Carrick in the early 1940s and outlived her husband, Tom Jordan, by many years. She took part in the RTÉ radio programme, 'The Story of Woodbrook', in 1986, in which the poet, Paul Durcan delivered the text as David Thomson. Tommy Maxwell, who recalled the Kirkwood years in the programme, died in 1990 and is buried in Ardcarne cemetery, very close, as it happens, to the old Kirkwood plot. The book also gave an impetus to the career of the musician, Micheál Ó Súilleabháin. He had performed a rearranged version of the hornpipe, 'The Plains of Boyle', for the programme, wistfully slowing the tune down. He later added orchestra for a successful recorded version, giving it the title 'Woodbrook'.

Tom Crowe, a native of County Clare and a student at Trinity College Dublin when he stayed at Woodbrook, went on to become a famous continuity announcer on the BBC Third Programme. He was one of the many rivals for

Phoebe's affections David had to endure. Tom's obituary in *The Irish Times* in December 2010 noted: 'While never openly rebellious, he managed to suggest a quiet, disingenuous dissidence, mildly sending up the BBC "grand manner" and himself with it.' He expressed bewilderment on air one time when Elgar's *Chanson de Matin* underran, not realizing the disc had been played at 45rpm, rather than 33rpm. On another occasion, when Mendelssohn's *Song Without Words* overran into the time signature 'pips', he announced to the listeners that he hoped the composer's work hadn't 'spoiled their enjoyment of the pips'. In the 1980s David exchanged letters with Julian Trevor-Roper, a son of Anthony Trevor Roper, another rival for her affections. He told David that his father and mother had enjoyed the book before his father's early death.

Woodbrook House still stands and its roof can be glimpsed through mature trees about three miles on the Boyle road from Carrick. John and Mai Malone bought it from the Maxwell brothers in 1970. They initially bought half the property, Jimmy Maxwell's, and moved into the house in 1974. Afterwards they bought Tommy's. They reared cattle on the approximately 200 acres that remained of the original estate. Over the years they willingly shared *Woodbrook* curiosity with the visitors who make the 'pilgrimage' to County Roscommon and stroll up the long avenue to see what remains of the legend. John remarked in a letter to David in 1978 that there were many people arriving over the years who felt they just had to see the house for themselves. He suggested that David might like to visit and even stay 'in his old bedroom'. Mai is well known locally as a singer.

In the 1980s John discovered one of the few photographs that exist of Phoebe Kirkwood in an outbuilding. John Malone died in October 2013, aged seventy-four. Like Mai, he was very conscious of the literary heritage of the house. He was quick witted, too: On 'The Story of Woodbrook', as he and Tommy Maxwell surveyed the two adjoining bedrooms that Thomson describes in the book, he asked a pertinent question:

– Tell me, Tommy, had she any other boyfriends – besides yourself?

Tommy replied:

– Oh, she was too much of a lady for the likes of me!

The Kilmacanogue Historical Society's chairman, Norman Colin, has enthusiastically chronicled that area's connection with the book, including the probable route taken by David and Phoebe through the tranquil grounds of the Jameson estate where they talked on a seat by the lily pond in 1943.

Rita Kiernan maintained an interest in all matters to do with *Woodbrook*, as her son Seán can testify. She told him the names of boyfriends Phoebe had while a student at Trinity. She liked to recall the Phoebe and David relationship – without revealing to her sons her own affair with him. He supposes the reason Rita speculated about Phoebe's sex life was because it concerned or had implications for her ex-lover, Seán concludes: 'One always keeps an interest in past affairs. It's just human nature.'

The Kirkwood family's presence in County Roscommon is now a faint memory, like that of the King-Harmons and the other Anglo-Irish families. Rockingham's parkland, dotted with its exotic trees, is a recreational facility for local people and holidaymakers. And Hughestown Hill, evoked in the book's opening page, has since been levelled by road construction. On the wall of the clubhouse at Carrick-on-Shannon Golf Club there's a picture of a man with a monocle, wearing plus-fours and a haughty expression. It's Charlie – Major Kirkwood – an early president of the club built on his land. And there's a lasting reminder of his family in Ardcarne Church, consecrated as the Church of Saint Beaidh, a stained-glass window by Evie Hone. The family commissioned it in David Thomson's time at Woodbrook, in 1935. It was one of Hone's earlier commissions, just before she converted from Anglicanism to Catholicism in 1937 and then dedicated her career to stained glass art. Like the east window of the church, it features Saint Beaidh, a local saint, but Hone's window, probably the finer, is facing north and doesn't get the same light.

A detail from the Evie Hone window at Saint Beidh's Church, Ardcarne.

Sylvia and Eddie Creighton are the present proprietors of Cryan's Bar on Bridge Street, Boyle. Sylvia can point to David Thomson's favourite spot at the bar. Cryan's traditional exterior has changed very little since David was a regular. From the bar, she says, he enjoyed keeping an eye on proceedings at fair days. Among the pub's memorabilia is a framed excerpt from *Woodbrook* where David describes Cryan's as his favourite place to drink in the town, and a print he always admired, two dogs happily playing.

David Thomson's favourite place to sit in Cryan's bar (courtesy Sylvia and Eddie Creighton).

The print on the wall in Cryan's that David Thomson particularly admired (courtesy Eddie and Sylvia Creighton).

In 1961, after the Thomsons bought their house near Edingthorpe in Norfolk, David insisted on making 'lazy beds' in the adjoining land. This was the folklorist and historian in him. He had discovered these characteristic ridges on the landscape and their historical significance at Woodbrook. Lazy beds were an ancient method of cultivation in Ireland and Scotland, where a series of ridges and troughs are dug. In Ireland they have a poignant history, as they were used during the Famine to try and cultivate the potato on hillsides where the crop wouldn't normally grow. A neighbour in Norfolk referred to this odd horticultural sight as 'your graves'.

And in the sitting room of a modern bungalow on the Carrick-on-Shannon Elphin Road, there is a large, interesting piece of furniture: Ivy Kirkwood's grand piano, a Schiedmayer from the famous Stuttgart makers. Children have practised their scales on it, unaware of the ghosts in its ivories.

The Schiedmayer piano said to be once owned by Ivy Kirkwood (courtesy Percy Carty).

13. The Great Hunger

A big project David undertook, as a BBC producer, was the story of the Irish Famine. The stark reality of it and the attitude of Ireland's rulers in London must have shocked many of his listeners. 'The Great Hunger', written and produced by him, was broadcast on the Third Programme on 22 March 1948, at 8.40 pm. It was a 55-minute 'drama documentary', another example of the Thomson confluence of fact and fiction, and included over fifty characters, from 'gombeen man' to Queen Victoria.

The narrator sets the scene, including this summary of the broader picture:

> By the standards of the time, immense efforts were made to contend with the terrible effects of famine. They failed. Some have blamed the landlords of Ireland for their callous indifference, some the ordinary people for their indolence, despair and inadaptability, and some have accused the British Government, which held power during those years.

He uses a rhyming game, heard off-microphone, as a counterpoint, in this scene from the programme.

CLANCY: I brought these couple of potatoes down, Martin, in the pocket here.

MARTIN: They're marked right enough, but that's no harm.

CLANCY: Take up the knife there and slice them.

MARTIN: It's kind of like a bruise on a man's face – de 'ye see it here over by the light, Tom Clancy – kind o' black and blue.

CLANCY: Slice it. EFFECT

MARTIN: Bigod – is there many more like that?

One of Thomson's sources was the testimony of Sarah Mahon, then eighty years old, from the Usna townland between Carrick-on-Shannon and Boyle, a place later to be made famous in *Woodbrook*. The programme ends with one of her recollections:

> If you look on Usna today, you'll see the way it was before the hand of God struck it. You'll see the green banks on every side that used to divide it into fine little gardens for potatoes, and where the cattle is grazing now you'll see ridges in the grass all up the hill, on every side, where the potatoes were planted a hundred years since and never dug. And now and again ploughing, ye might find the coulter o' the plough stuck in the foundations of a house that stood there, before the Great Hunger.

David's interest in the subject continued as he wrote *Woodbrook;* in fact, it nearly caused the abandoning of the project, as he got overwhelmed with the detailed research he'd done and couldn't find a satisfactory way he thought of cutting it down.

While researching 'The Great Hunger,' he had come across the diaries of Elizabeth Smith, a nineteenth-century landowner, of the Baltiboys estate on the River Liffey near Blessington, County Wicklow. She kept a detailed diary of life in this part of Ireland for forty-five years. David co-edited her record of the years 1840 to 1850 with Moyra McGusty, a great granddaughter of Smith. Clarendon Press, Oxford, published *The Irish Journals of Elizabeth Smith 1840-1850* in 1980.

The Baltiboys estate suffered its own unique fate in 1939 and much of it is now under water as part of the Poulaphouca reservoir. The nearby An Óige hostel was once a school founded by Elizabeth Smith.

The Smith story pressed several buttons for Thomson; it was an Anglo-Irish story; it was an historical subject he'd already researched; there was a strong Scottish connection and similarities between Smith's and his own background. She was a Grant, born in Edinburgh in 1797, who spent some of her early years in India. With David the process was, of course the 'reverse'. He discovered Elizabeth Smith could read at the age of three, and recite long ballads. Like he a century later, she overcame illness and taught herself to write.

There was also a parallel with David's mother's life, as both women went to India for marriage reasons. Elizabeth Smith says of the year 1828, 'Everybody was busy marrying me.' Like Annie Thomson and Ivy Kirkwood also, she found a match in the British military. In her case it was a Colonel Henry Smith, whose family had the lands in County Wicklow.

She refers to her husband throughout the book as The Colonel, treating him with a mixture of reverence and occasionally condescension: in 1847 there was a right-of-way issue she decided to deal with herself rather than let him 'get upset' and bring on a cough as he suffered from asthma most of his life. The diaries are extensive and this period of ten years included in *The Irish Journals of Elizabeth Smith* runs to over 200 pages, containing detailed accounts of tenants' family disputes, passing her own judgments on their financial and moral behaviour, and suggesting courses of action to a particular party.

Wicklow was less affected by the potato failure than other parts of Ireland, but the diaries catalogue great misery and death. The Smiths did take some measures to alleviate the calamity around them; one was to import rice and Indian meal directly from England so it could be available at a lower price. But their charity had boundaries. 'Example does much and as we can't assist all we must only continue to look after our own and be content to distribute elsewhere the crumbs left by those who have a right to the bread.'

Thomson points out that Smith was actually proud of resorting to eviction, justifying it by persuading herself, as many landowners did, that the land could not support so many people. And he gets almost angry with this long-dead woman and her imperious ways, which he otherwise admires in so many respects:

> How can she vituperate against the Irish for their laziness when there was no employment to be had, nor, once the potato crop had failed, any work to be done on their small holdings? How complain when they preferred to beg or die at home rather than go into the poorhouse, when her husband, who was a Poor Law Guardian, must have known how overcrowded it was?

A photo of David Thomson, early 1980s (courtesy Martina Thomson).

In a diary entry for May 1848, there's an insight into her political view as she speaks a little scornfully of the rebel paper, *The United Irishman*. The Smiths had it brought to the house to keep in touch, as it were, with rebellious thinking, but there wasn't always an edition: 'Last week no printer would work for these madmen. They have found someone to spread their treason this week.' Yet she goes on to regard a letter to the paper as being full of sense and says that the authorities should heed what the writer says. She then mentions a recent meeting of *Protestant repealers* (her emphasis): 'These are calm, clear, steady men of business,' she says, 'who a year ago would have treated repeal [of the Act of Union] as the wildest of all crazy things'.

The Smiths, while doing much to relieve starvation, nonetheless lived a high life themselves during the Famine period. But Thomson reminds us of the smugness of our own time: 'When we read of banquets in Blessington and Dublin, during the worst years of the Great Famine, we should remember that we ourselves feast while we look at the pictures of the victims of famine on our TV screens.'

Maeve Kennedy, reviewing *The Irish Journals of Elizabeth Smith* in *The Irish Times* in March 1980, notes that Smith wrote the journals for 'her dear little daughters' and concludes she was 'a good woman, but a peculiarly Victorian one'. David Thomson's seems to share an openness of personality and a measure of his characteristics as a writer with Elizabeth Smith, as he concludes in the book's introduction: 'Like anyone else's her mind is filled with contradictory notions and desires. These and several opposing traits of her character appear because she uses no disguises. She puts everything truthfully as it occurred to her at the moment. In most considered books, such opposites are hidden from the reader.'

In *Woodbrook*, he goes back to this period of Irish history in Chapter 8, inviting the reader across the bridge in Carrick-on-Shannon where he says the Shannon 'shines like gun-metal in cloudy weather and on clear days is blue like a calm sea bay', to some old buildings in the town with a dark past – they were once one of the largest workhouses in Ireland. He relates a controversy that occurred at the height of the Famine in 1848 when the Inspector of the institution, Captain Wynne, was accused of improper conduct against a local woman. Thomas Kirkwood, a relation of the Woodbrook Kirkwoods, whose house was at Clongoonagh, a mile nearer Carrick, made the complaint against him. Thomson gives a detailed account of proceedings in which Kirkwood complained to Wynn's superiors, the Poor Law Commissioners in Dublin. The complaint then ended up in the House of Lords, an investigation proceeded, and witnesses were called to London in 1850. These buildings in Carrick-on-Shannon became a *cause célebre*.

Thomson is convinced that the core of the accusation was hearsay evidence against Wynne, who, he says, was actually pro-active in attempting to relieve starvation in Carrick and Boyle. There was a conflict between him as 'chief executive' and the 'board', the Poor Law guardians, composed of local gentry, including James Kirkwood of Woodbrook. The case for the prosecution was financial irregularities and misconduct of a sexual nature by Wynne. The defence was that Wynne was doing his best in the dire conditions that prevailed, and that the number of starving people under his care swelled from 350 in November 1847 to 1900. Thomson comments that working for long hours every day among the dead and dying, fraud, debt or any financial irregularities must have seemed to Wynne the least of evils.

As for the alleged sexual impropriety, Thomson reveals a very grim side to the story. Helpless pauper women, desperate to secure passage to Australia, had only one form of bribery at their disposal. In the case of a woman who was admitted to Carrick workhouse in 1846, Catherine Foley, and about whom Wynne was questioned and for whom he secured passage to Australia, the enquiry established that he knew her better than he admitted. Was he taking advantage, or was it a consensual relationship? Certainly his position of power over her and all the others cannot be ignored in any judgment. Was Thomson, to some extent, being too understanding of a man who loved a much younger woman in his care?

The Lords' report severely criticized Captain Wynne but he was not dismissed from the Poor Law service. The Kirkwood brothers and their fellow guardians were censored but remained in office. Thomson, having studied all the evidence, considered the conclusions fair. But the most remarkable feature of the report, he writes, is that in all its pages there is no mention of the famine itself: 'The omission of that dreaded word tells another truth. It is the key to government policy enacted by Lord John Russell, the Prime Minister, who in spite of plentiful evidence to the contrary stuck to the theory that Ireland should look after itself – a policy that was the cause of millions of unnecessary deaths.'

David Thomson would be pleased to see the Famine memorial that now stands in Ardcarne churchyard. It's the work of the sculptor Jackie McKenna and was erected in 1997.

For his next book, however, David stayed local.

The Famine memorial by Jackie McKenna at Ardcarne Church.

14. In Camden Town

In March 1976 the editor of the *Camden Journal* received a letter from an irate resident, complaining about a new official notice that had appeared in public lavatories in the borough: 'No Shaving'. The complainant wasn't a homeless person, the editor discovered, but clearly someone with a literary bent; he referred to Banquo's ghost and quoted a famous former councillor who had campaigned successfully for women's toilets in the area in the early twentieth century, George Bernard Shaw. Camden Council was being admonished with gusto. The writer continued:

> What harm do the present day Bumbledons [derogatory term for council officials] attribute to shaving at the miserable little basin in Mornington Crescent, usually soap less, which they provide? I know dozens of homeless men in Camden Town where I live who are refused service in certain shops because they look dirty and unshaven. Those who prefer to grow beards fare better.

Then he adds a more personal note, revealing something of himself: 'When my job involved night journeys from Scotland and Ireland, I often arrived too late to go home and shave before getting to my office. There are thousands like me.'

The letter came from 22 Regent's Park Terrace; the writer was a certain David Thomson, associated with the Camden Town area since 1955. His reflections on the area and the time he spent here since 1955, as well as his internal struggles, are the subject of *In Camden Town*, published by Hutchinson in hardback, and Penguin, in 1983. The years since *Woodbrook* hadn't been greatly productive for David and his anguish about this is at the core of the book.

In August 1980, according to the diary form the book takes, David is visiting his doctor, a Dr Haas. He's explaining that he's finding it difficult to make progress on the writing. He tells the doctor he doesn't write for money or hope of fame, but for itself. But the mood that he had since childhood where he could write under any conditions seems remote from him now. The doctor responded:

> But you are going on with your diary?
>
> And I told him, yes, not every day but more and more, that it's better than the abyss of last year but it's not the book. I described the book as a monstrous growth on the brain; often the thought of it makes me physically sick. I can't get rid of it. Nor can I write it.

But Thomson did, of course, complete his literary evocation of Camden – the streetscapes, the people, and the natural environment of a London borough.

The Thomsons' home, 22 Regent's Park Terrace, Camden Town.

Recalling the background to their move to this area, Martina said David always liked beautiful rooms, adding that he didn't always care how he lived in them. 'I first slept under his blankets at 33 Portland Place, these were a cobweb of rags, and blankets of dust covered the floor and the furniture.'

She remembers a grand roll-top desk. In this room there was also a flowered bidet. He shared this flat with Michael Wharton, one of his Oxford friends, also a writer. She echoed her own past: 'What seemed strange to me was that Michael denied his Jewishness; his real name had been Michael Nathan and I believe his son went back to that surname.'

In the summer of 1955, after David had made the programme about the song tradition in Lapland, and he and Martina had returned to London, they began to look for a house to buy. David's father had died in 1953 and David inherited £300 from his estate. Martina's mother offered to lend them some money. So, with only a small mortgage, they found a bijou residence in Lancaster Gate. When she showed it to a friend, he shook his head and showed her a place opposite in dire condition, 22 Regent's Park Terrace. They just fell for it. It was the elegance of the rooms, she said. The house was rewired and decorated at the seller's expense as part of the deal.

While this was going on, Timothy, Martina's first son, was born on 17 September 1955. David had asked his landlord whether they might stay on, but he said: 'Out, out!', according to Martina. They were an unmarried couple and she was visibly pregnant.

When Martina came out of The Middlesex Hospital, they went to stay with her mother and in March 1956 moved into 22 Regent's Park Terrace. David's workroom was quickly established, but their kitchen was upstairs as they had to let out the large downstairs room that later became the kitchen, first to Margaret Gardner, friend of many artists, then Louis MacNeice and his lover at the time, the actress, Mary Wimbush, who had a part for many years in *The Archers* on BBC Radio 4; then to Merlyn Evans as a studio for seven years. The basement was always let – this was factored in as an income in Martina's calculations.

The early-nineteenth-century house has a wealth of architectural features. The previous owner was a well-known stained-glass craftsman, Charles Moore, responsible for many church windows around Britain. The staircase of number 22 is lit by one of his windows.

The street is tranquil now, a desirable and exclusive neighbourhood. The soot from steam trains and the smoke that David recalls in *In Camden Town*, are long gone. Modern trains whizz by in a cutting behind a wall, almost unnoticed. Thomson describes the trauma caused by the railway being mercilessly cut through this area in Dickens's time by the London and Birmingham Railway Company, causing loss of life among the huge labour force needed to extend the line from its earlier terminus at Camden right down to Euston. An Act of Parliament was required to allow this huge engineering project. One of the buildings demolished was a school once attended by Dickens, Mr Jones's Classical and Commercial Academy. Thomson finds a reference in the writer's work: 'A great trunk line had swallowed the playground, sliced away the schoolroom, and pared off the corner of the house: which, thus curtailed of its proportions, presented itself, in a green stage of stucco, profile wise towards the road, like a forlorn flatiron without a handle, standing on end.'*

He describes holding his children up to see over the bridge at Oval Road in the early 1960s and watch the trains heading north, their shape emerging from the smoke that enveloped everyone on the bridge. 'We watched the long train until we could no longer see it. It climbed the hill slowly. The trains fill my heart with restless longings to this day.'

Trains had always been a feature of Thomson's life, this line particularly. On these same tracks he had travelled nearly 500 miles to Inverness and Nairn as a child, or to Holyhead to catch the boat to Ireland as an adult.

In 1955 the Thomsons moved into pre-gentrification Camden. 'It's a vastly different Camden Town now,' says Luke Dodd, who rented their basement for several years and still lives locally. 'All the Irish navvies who could be seen hanging out at the Tube station are gone. The area is unrecognizable. All the roughness has been laundered out of the place.'

Dylan Thomas lived, for a period, close to David's favourite pub, The Edinburgh Castle. The novelist Beryl Bainbridge was a Camden resident for most of David's time there. She was born in 1932 and died in 2010; shortlisted for the Booker Prize five times, she won the Whitbread Prize twice. Her 1989 novel, *An Awfully Big Adventure*, was adapted to a film in 1995, starring Alan Rickman and Hugh Grant. Bainbridge had a colourful, turbulent life as borne out by the meeting that David recounts in *In Camden Town*. They were discussing their children when she met him as he sat outside having a drink. Her

* Charles Dickens, *Household Words*, Volume 4, 1851.

fifteen-year-old daughter, she recounted, had drunk a cup of vodka, fallen off a bus and cracked her skull: 'a whole cup and fell off the bus. She's perfectly all right. She came home from hospital, dyed her hair green and off again.'

Then he introduces his two homeless friends, Davy and Mary. Both were Scottish, an important point for David. They had met one Christmas Eve in 1969 when Davey came up to him saying the off licence was shut and could he go into the pub for him and get some cider. David obliged, bought cider – and Guinness for himself, then the two hobos and the writer from the posh house went to drink together on a nearby bench. David discovered that he and Davy had spent much of their childhood in the same part of Scotland, miles apart socially. Davy knew the Nairn harbour well, used to land fresh fish in time for the night train to London. David remembered how his own grandmother used to harangue the fishmonger saying that his fish was yesterday's. 'All the fresh fish goes to London,' she used to say.

The relationship lasted for the remainder of Thomson's life and included occasional hospitality at Regent's Park Terrace. Tim Thomson remembers the time he was asked to make a sandwich for them and while he was in the kitchen, Mary disappeared with Martina's coat. The coat was recovered, though so damaged that Martina never wore it again, though the friendship survived the incident. Davy came from a traveller family, spoke the travellers' language with Mary and switched to English when he remembered David didn't understand. Mary had been married once, but now had an on-off relationship with Davy.

David suggests there were other people inside each of them trying to get out of wretched bodies and circumstances, capable of a life that might have been. He recounts a visit by Mary to number 22 where he asked her was she still taking her pills:

> She showed them to me a fortnight ago, taking them out of her small plastic bag, a spongebag she had found, blue and pretty. That was why she showed them. She wanted me to look into it and see her hairbrush, mirror, and face cream – surprisingly dainty things. Now she had lost the bag and the pills with it.

Luke Dodd sums up this aspect of David: 'He was a true egalitarian. It was innate in him.' His appearance, too, meant he didn't stand out from his dispossessed friends. Martina recalled a time when David was refused admission to a

London steak house and was very indignant. In the book he recounts how he had to leave a performance of *Educating Rita* in the Piccadilly Theatre because he couldn't hear. He was wandering about when a little Indian boy tapped him on the arm and pressed 20p into his hand. He was trying to give it back when the boy's father said, 'take it'. So he took it politely and said he'd remember it all his life, which he did. A similar indication of David's physical appearance comes from the fact that on one of David's return visits to Nairn, he was refused admission to Newton, his mother's family's home, then a hotel.

David Gentleman, who provided the cover illustration for *In Camden Town*, admits that some of David's local friends he would have regarded as faintly undesirable, 'But that wouldn't have entered David's head.' Did Gentleman approve of his friend's choice? His answer is emphatic: 'I approved of everything David did.' Gentleman and his first wife, Rosalind Dease, met the Thomsons when they first arrived in the street. When both couples agreed to take down the wire that separated their back gardens; their friendship was sealed symbolically.

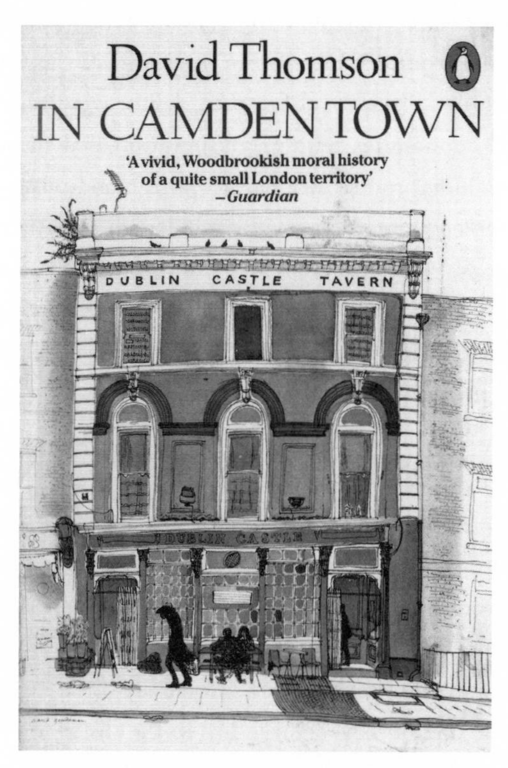

The cover of In Camden Town, *featuring a drawing by David Gentleman of one of David's favourite Camden pubs*

Luke Thomson describes his father as something of a loner once he had left his BBC career behind. The book does suggest a certain solitariness, a preoccupation with writing and lack of writing; the melancholy creeping into the pages. This is evident in David's thoughts about his relationship with Davie Laing, a resident of Arlington House, the large homeless hostel in Camden Town. Regret sets in on a bleak day as he makes the journey to Laing's funeral at St Pancras Cemetery, at a public grave with few mourners. He is overcome with remorse. Had he been neglectful? Even though they were never very close, they had shared so much time together in the Edinburgh Castle and loved its garden in summer. They both suffered eyesight problems and melancholia. Their conditions kept them apart when it could have brought them together, he thinks. Should he have learned more about the man while he was alive, just like he should have more enquiring of his own father, who had died thirty years before, he wonders?

This part of *In Camden Town* is another meditation on the chemistry of friendship. An intellectual bond went beyond the talk accompanying their many pints of bitter. Both men read, David more than Davie, but Thomson notes that it was Davie who reintroduced him to the stories from the Old Testament, the stories of Cain and Abel, Jacob and Esau and Ruth, which David put to use in *Dandiprat's Days*. He concludes with an observation that demonstrates his ear for dialect: 'He reminded me of all I had forgotten and when bringing ancient names to life, his voice slowed down, his Edinburgh accent took on a tinge of Highland because it was from his Highland grandmother that he first heard these stories told.'

Thomson recalls Davie's pride made him use the Arlington House street number, 220 Arlington Rd., rather than the name of the hostel itself. He longed to return to his native Edinburgh and Leith, but when he did make the journey he found Edinburgh was like a 'ghost town' and Leith 'quite dead'. The 'ghosts' were of course the ghosts of his own years there that he was lamenting. He had built 'a dream of contentment that was only a dream', a recurring theme in writing as apparently far apart as Dónal Mac Amhlaigh's *Dialann Deoraí* and Gerry Rafferty's song, 'Baker Street'.

In Camden Town has glimpses of the emotional life of 22 Regent's Park Terrace. One day he and Martina observe a large fire in the distance at Paddington. The smoke darkened the sky and he describes a doomsday feeling, and a more troubling memory. They are reminded of the last great smog that occurred in London, when Martina was with another man, 'the smog – how she was excited by it, enjoyed it, and how doom-like I felt it to be because I knew she was with him'.

Thomson can make ordinary tasks, the domestic drudgery familiar to most people, seem curiously reflective. He did this in *Woodbrook* with the butter churn. Here he has an almost psychedelic description of a launderette.

> Some stare at their washing swirling around with a TV expression, in a dull acceptance of whatever it is you're given to watch ... In the dryer which has a larger screen and no interference from soap, I watched Ben's trousers chasing Martina's shirt; reds, blues, yellows, white streamers from the ribbon of her nightdress, dark blotches of my jeans, all flying in a circle, blown by the fiery wind.

He also describes what he calls Martina's 'pyromania', the way a simple bonfire could completely absorb her. He found the same fascination in the work of Maxim Gorki, a reference to 'the smoky air that tears one's lungs, yet one feels strangely unwilling to go'. He recalls seeing Martina stay up half the night at bonfires she'd made in the country, 'Yet she kept putting new things on and whenever I came out to see her long after dark on summer nights her eyes were on fire, but she looked serious and peaceful like a religieuse in silent hidden ecstasy.'

Observing the seasons is another Thomson talent. In his entry for 4 May 1980, the subject is the power of the cherry blossom. The pink is floating in the streets when he notices some children outside a Japanese school. Japanese culture has a centuries-old practice of picnicking under a blooming sakura, or cherry tree, during the fleeting annual appearance of that great blossom. He imagines – and convinces Martina momentarily – that the children, sons and daughters of ex pats, are throwing the blossoms in some form of spring ceremony.

Writing block and its associated moods recurs in *In Camden Town*. Andrew Hoellering, Martina's cousin, remembers casually asking David during this time 'how the book was going'. The writer flew into a rage, apparently; It was a sensitive matter. Inability to write and the depression that comes with it creates a vicious circle that causes emptiness and gloom.

He describes a consultation with Dr Haas where the doctor suggested that David wasn't dealing well with the idea of getting old, that he wasn't accepting it, that he must realize that he couldn't be as quick and spontaneous as he used to be. But that didn't mean that his faculties, or his power as a writer were diminished. This was reassuring. Then the doctor asked him if he'd experienced a block during *Woodbrook.* Yes, he had nearly given up. He thought at the time that it was because of the chapter about the Famine, all the detailed research had made him weary and couldn't see how to cut it down. David told the doctor that he now believes the block began with a mood rather than a practical difficulty.

Then Dr Haas asked him to describe the other mood – the one that leads to fluid writing. David said it was about self-confidence, a lack of self-criticism *while* writing; it's all right then to cross out what you've done next day, or even hate what you've written. You try to get into what he calls 'a deeper layer'. You know you're there when you're able to recall forgotten dreams. And there may be activity around you – traffic, children playing, but you're immune to these interruptions when you reach this state. 'More importantly you are removed from the bitty scraps on the surface of your mind.'

Dr Silvio Benaim, David Thomson's psychiatrist, had prescribed different medications over the years. In the book David describes the effects of Tofranil and Tryptizol, both tricyclic anti-depressants, or, more importantly for him, the fact that he had to give up drinking while he was on them. It's a discussion about the pros and cons of medication, its real or perceived effect on creativity, which continues to the present day. Such medications, as well as Lithium, were part of most of David's adult life. David Gentleman, who knew David well for many years, didn't notice any dramatic effects during his friend's low moods. His own father-in-law, George Ewart Evans, had suffered what's called 'the black dog', so Gentleman thought it was 'par for the course'.

There's joy in this chronicle, but sadness too: brightly expressed sadness. Winter setting in; descriptions of dying elm trees near his house. He recounts a routine melancholy, a gloom he feels after seeing Martina to Finchley Road station one day. 'All the way back I tried to follow our footsteps, crossing the road where we had crossed.' There's an echo here of an early passage in *Woodbrook* the first summer he arrived and Phoebe is showing him the well and the small stream that runs from it. After they both drink from the water, he sentimentally imagines how long might it take for the water she touched to flow into the Shannon.

Romance comes in more robust form, too. When he's unhappy, he confesses, all attractive women go into hiding. But when he's happy they emerge from hibernation, like spring flowers in the snow: 'But you must not pick them.'

When he gets on a bus he admits to choosing to sit beside the prettiest head of hair he can see. Then comes another *In Camden Town* admission:

> Once some such beauty tossed her hair back and it fell over my arms, which were bare in short sleeves. It was one of those rare hot days. Hair has no feeling in it. It only hurts if you pull. I pushed the rest gently towards her neck and stroked the part she had given to me. Assault, I suppose, in legal terms.

He recalls a time he was staying with Seamus and Marie Heaney at their home in Dublin. Seamus brought him to the local literary landmark, Joyce's Tower. They walked to the bathing place beside it; where in *Ulysses* Buck Mulligan teases Stephen Dedalus as he shaved himself by a rock. David thought the rocks were exceptionally sexual in shape. Heaney remarked on it too.

> I said
>
> – Almost every object is sexy.
>
> – Yes, thank God, Seamus said.

There were many newspaper reviews of *In Camden Town*, thanks to David Thomson's strong reputation since *Woodbrook*. Sheila McLeod reviewed the book in the *Evening Standard*, calling its account of the district 'quirkily original', and concluding:

> What connects the disparate elements is a pervasive awareness of change and death. But, thanks to David Thomson's rigorous emotional honesty and to his idiosyncratic eye and ear for detail, whether in the streets or in his reading, the result is not nostalgia. It is a ragbag transformed into a treasury by a loving but realistic process of selection.

Terence de Vere White wrote a long review for *The Spectator* in 1983. He said Thomson had never obtruded but 'brings up the sensitive rear'. He has gone among the down and outs 'with the patience of a wildlife naturalist'. But then he touches on what for many readers is a weakness: 'Mr Thomson has disinterred a great mass of fascinating material … but if the book has a flaw it is self-indulgence in the use of this ingredient.' He concluded by returning to *Woodbrook*:

> A deceptively quiet book, so quiet it presented a threat to reviewers in a hurry; so easy, if one were tired and not attending properly, to have let it slip by in the crowd. As I recall it got off to a slow start to become – to give it the trade name – a minor classic. When a writer pulls off that kind of book – as difficult as it is for a hen to lay a square egg – he is pestered for the rest of his life to do it again.

David Thomson at the bar of The Dublin Castle, Parkway, Camden Town, on the occasion of the publication of In Camden Town *(courtesy David Gentleman).*

The tone of Frank Delaney's review in *The Sunday Press* implies *Woodbrook* was a hard act to follow, as he takes up half the review in praising the earlier work. Yet his mixed conclusion would still be the envy of many a writer:

> His stature is not Shakespearean. He is not memorable for his brilliance of ideas or his exposition of intellectual force. But he has one gift that is a great gift. In recounting the life in the world he has known or now lives in, he creates another world, a world of frail human beings, in short, the world we all inhabit ourselves.

'A terrific book about a writing block' was how Seamus Heaney described *In Camden Town* when he chose to read from the book at the memorial in Dublin a year after David's death. 'It's full of its own problems, but delivers itself successfully in the end'.

He chose the diary entry that concludes the book, an image that's completely ordinary, of a lost glove blowing about in the Tube station. 'This wonderful inner image of the spirit, as Eliot says, "unappeased and peregrine", just floating, completely susceptible, completely open and alive.'

Thomson was watching the man in uniform sweeping the floor of the station on Good Friday night, gathering rubbish with a wide broom, the abandoned debris of the day, when he saw the glove.

> I expected him to pick it up, as I would have – I thought of picking it up but I was too late. He smothered it in a wide sweep. It seemed to me extraordinary and shocking that he had no feeling for it. Several images went through my mind, a symbolic hand, a dead blackbird, an ornamental bookmark fallen from a lectern Bible – any once-precious relic being tumbled in the dirt. As I went up the escalator I remembered the Tatterdemalion whom I haven't seen for months and thought of his body, if he were to die in the Tube, being tumbled about with the rest of the thrown-away rubbish.

Jeananne Crowley was a successful screen and television actress in her thirties when she got to know David and Martina, after her *Woodbrook* review. She often went drinking with him on occasions in The Edinburgh Castle, in the years before *In Camden Town*. David, it seems, was politely flirtatious: 'I think he fancied the proverbial pants off me. I was under no illusion that the reason he sought out my company was entirely to do with my prowess as a reviewer, as much as the fact that I was, back then, young, pretty and full of enthusiasm for him.' She remembers that the pub had a large mirror and seeing her once check her reflection in it, David said: 'One should always have a mirror in life that reflects you beautifully, Jeananne, even if you don't need one, but especially if, like me, you do.'

She also muses on David's friendship with Heaney: 'They were cut from same corner of the tablecloth really, though David didn't possess even an ounce of Heaney's resilience or ability to deal with quotidian reality. He was less anchored than most and found the business of being a human a serious trial at times.'

15. County Clare Interlude

David took a dislike to the woman who ran a bed and breakfast in Ballyvaughan, her curlers, and particularly her bungalow. He kept a diary during his and Martina's summer holiday in West Clare in 1982.

When Martina asked why he complained so much, he replied that the lady had been fitted out 'by some company that offers the petit nouveau bourgeoisie inclusive terms, on easy payments, and includes a glass boat for a milk jug, shiny barometer with matching clock for the hall'. His critique may ring true for anyone who experienced this kind of accommodation in Ireland in the 1970s and 1980s. He continues, castigating the woman's taste in 'art': 'On the wall, a picture of a white ship on blue sea, with matching white horses on crests of waves, all constructed out of wire.'

The Thomsons went out for a walk and when they returned the door was shut, so they rang the bell. 'I couldn't hear it, but Martina said it did the right thing – ding-dong chimes!'

Thomson had commented on aesthetic matters before. He once made a parable out of one such observation: In his introduction to the first edition of *The*

People of the Sea he describes a visit to Dublin in the early 1950s, where a friend brought him to see the newly opened Merrion Square. 'Go and see it', the friend said, 'before the gardeners get in with their tulips!' David thought modernity and conformity for their own sake wasn't a good idea. Moving on to folklore and his experiences in the west of Ireland, he derides the tendency, he observes, to either obliterate or at least overlook the past, and to denigrate or even dismiss the oral folklore tradition. On reaching the West 'he feared that the cultural gardeners might have reached it with concrete symmetry at their heels'. In Fitzwilliam Square that unspoilt time, the trees were 'beautifully untended', the lawn 'more like a meadow'.

Thirty years later he was delighted to discover the wild grounds of the Falls Hotel, including the river Inagh's cascades, when staying in the village of Ennistymon. There was a connection here with his one-time BBC associate and Camden neighbour Dylan Thomas, whose wife, Caitlín McNamara, came from the family who owned the house for over a century. David liked the trees and shrubs, but criticized the hotel for 'turning one beautiful room into three biscuit tins'. Martina said she'd rather be in Edingthorpe, they had a holiday row, and then harmony was restored.

The Thomsons during this holiday were engaging in a form of transport that's now virtually extinct – hitch hiking. They didn't want to walk towards Lahinch because the cars 'would be whizzing round our ankles', so they took the back road to Liscannor, where a car stopped and brought them to the Cliffs of Moher. Thomson looked out at the Aran Islands and recalled his first time there in 1947, when Ernie O'Malley brought him. Then Martina discovered that a blue-bottle had got into the bag with their sandwiches, so she gave them all to the seabirds.

They had pints in a grocer's shop in Liscannor, whose conviviality caused reflections that David recorded that evening. He thought that the shop with its dim light and earthiness must be unchanged since long before his Woodbrook years. The quiet atmosphere and gentle murmur of people brought him back at once to Henry's bar in Cootehall, then to memories of Cryan's in Boyle and his Carrick-on-Shannon haunts. 'I didn't say anything at first, but Martina knew what I was feeling. I tried to explain that it was a happy feeling, not nostalgia or sadness, or wanting my own youth back.'

David's diary takes a more polemical turn as this train of thought reminds him of another writer, Maurice Leitch. Leitch had joined the BBC just as David was retiring in 1969. In 1977 Leitch became editor of 'A Book at Bedtime' on Radio 4 until leaving in 1989 to write full-time. His career pattern had similarities with David's. David is annoyed because Leitch had apparently counted him among English people who wrote about Ireland in comments he had made, believing David saw Ireland his 'in the rosy glow the past takes on for some people'.

Maurice Leitch had been awarded the Whitbread Prize a year previously in 1981 for his novel, *Silver's City*. Whether artistic jealousy or envy at the award had played some part (Thomson had yet to receive a literary honour), he abandoned his normal gentleness to criticize Leitch's work: 'Read 28 pages, glanced through the rest. No imagination, no poetry, clickety-clackety sudden full stop style ... worse than boring, crude and ugly.'

In the pub in Liscannor he and Martina had another couple of pints and Martina wondered, he wrote in his diary, what is the quality of life here that it differs so much from England. 'Why do English people dislike or even hate Irish people when they possess the qualities they admire – gentleness, good manners and an absence of vulgarity.'

The Thomsons' relationship with Ireland over the years included a friendship with the essayist and scholar, Hubert Butler, a native of Bennettsbridge, County Kilkenny. During 1977 David used what influence he had with various London publishers seeking to have Butler's later highly regarded work, *Ten Thousand Saints*, then out of print, republished. In a letter to David in October 1977 Butler describes moving house as like what Sean O'Casey's character Fluther Good described as a 'state of chassis'. He mentions writing to the publishers Thames & Hudson, citing Thomson's admiration of *Ten Thousand Saints.*

Butler's enquiring mind, knowledge of the Anglo-Irish psyche and passion for history were very appealing to Thomson. And Butler had another attraction: he was another man of the soil, having been a market gardener.

The Wellbrook Press in Kilkenny first published *Ten Thousand Saints* in 1972. Thomson became an admirer of its radical thesis, criticized at the time, that the accepted history of the Irish saints and their relationship to Europe was flawed. Alan Harrison (1943–2005), Professor of Irish at University College, Dublin, wrote an introduction to the book for Lilliput Press edition in 2005, in which he confesses to once being a critic of Butler. In the revised edition he elevates the scholar over what he refers to as 'so called Celtic spirituality'. Butler had termed his approach 'country scholarship' as opposed to trained scholarship. This would have appealed to Thomson. Butler was saying that a culturally national approach wasn't the right one and argued that the saints of Ireland were disguised personifications of the tribes and political factions of Iron Age Ireland. That's why we have so many: 'ten thousand'.

The Butlers knew Pamela Travers, the creator of *Mary Poppins*, through a boy they fostered, Joseph Hone, one of whose brothers, Camillus, had been adopted by Travers. The boys' parents, Nathaniel and Biddy Hone had strangely given away all their seven children. The learned atmosphere at Maindnhall was a factor that inspired Little Joe, as he was known, to later become a successful writer. He told his story in his memoir, *Wicked Little Joe* (2009).

The Thomsons stayed in County Kilkenny several times with Hubert and his wife, Peggy, a sister of the actor Tyrone Guthrie of Annaghmakerrig, County Monaghan, whose house became a writers' retreat, the Tyrone Guthrie Centre. Butler wrote to David in September 1978 to say that the art collectors, Sir Alfred and Lady Clementine Beit, would join them for dinner on their next visit, the year that the Beits had given their home, Russborough House, to the Irish people.

Following his *Woodbrook* success, David was invited to read at Kilkenny Arts Week that autumn. He chose extracts from *The People of the Sea*, *Dandiprat's Days* and two from *Woodbrook*. One of these was the same passage Seamus Heaney had chosen for the RTÉ 's 'Imprint' in 1975. This is where David, who himself was so often troubled at night, observes his employer Charlie Kirkwood's nocturnal habits, and instead of being alarmed by the man's tea-making and pipe-smoking in the dead of night, the young David 'envied his extraordinary composure'.

Thomson here is unintentionally embracing all who are denied, for whatever reasons, the comfort of healthy sleep. There are many references to nocturnal turmoil in his work, from cool Roscommon nights to writings in the sweaty tropics. His Liberian diary, written while he worked there on secondment to UNESCO from BBC in 1954, expressed insomnia's turmoil imaginatively:

> All night beautiful rain and frogs –now I find them friendly but don't sleep for long and still start the lunatic thoughts if I stay in bed awake for long, so I've seen a lot of early mornings…the most mysterious time is about 4, movement and rustling gradually growing, birds calling and re-assuring each other …

In that diary, incidentally, Thomson is trying to get to grips with the complex colonial situation in East Africa and at the same time being tantalized by the local womenfolk. He describes them physically in great detail, their curves, their lips, and their breast shape.

But on this holiday in 1982, we find a more mature David, quite frail for his age, though his wild side not completely tamed, as friends have testified. He still liked a pint, but also an early night – at the United Arts Club, just off Baggot Street, where he often stayed on Dublin visits.

Coincidentally, only weeks after that 1982 visit by the Thomsons, a connection with David's BBC and folklore past ended when Séamus Ennis became ill an died at his home in The Naul, County Dublin, aged sixty-three. Most of the BBC hard-living features men, with their colourful lives driven by great drinking sessions, were no more, in most cases outlived by their spouses. Another colleague, Philip Donnellan, in his 1988 unpublished autobiography, has a reference to Séamus Ennis's death that perhaps sums up nature's payback for the lifestyles of men like Eric Ewens, Louis MacNeice and Dylan Thomas: 'He's dead now, his gaunt frame, like a clothesline supporting a battered grey suit, eventually gave out and two thousand people came to his funeral in Dublin.'*

And now time was catching up on another of their number.

---

* Philip Donnellan, *We Were the BBC*, 1988 (www.philipdonnellan.co.uk).

16. A Roscommon Coda

David Thomson made his last visit to Ireland in the summer of 1987. Luke Dodd, then curator of Strokestown House, had invited him to perform the official opening of the house in June. David, aged seventy-three, had become quite frail. Luke Dodd remembers picking him and Martina up at Dublin Airport. He recalls the sight of an elderly man emerging eventually through arrivals when it seemed everyone else from the flight had long since departed. At the event itself in Strokestown, he became weak during his speech and Martina had to take over the reading of his script – a recollection of his own relationship with the house and a meditation on the significance of the country's Anglo-Irish heritage.

His script recalled the first time he was brought here by the Kirkwoods in 1932, how intimidated he felt meeting the Packenham-Mahons, until Phoebe and the Packenham-Mahon's daughter Lattice, whose 'Chinese-looking eyes' fascinated him, took him out to play in the grounds.

> I think that Phoebe then, when she was nearing her twelfth birthday, took charge of me – almost bossed me about – except during lessons when I took

> charge. Her mother certainly thought so, because later on that summer, when the Packenham-Mahons were expected to spend the day at Woodbrook, she told Phoebe in my presence not to keep on calling me to her as though I was her favourite dog.

He went on to talk about the prominence of Strokestown House in the layout of the village, comparing it to Oscar Wilde's Selfish Giant's house, its entrance dominating the street. He called it an 'aggressive magnificence' and a symbol of 'private dictatorship':

> I mention this because I believe no one should forget the past. When you visit the Tower of London ... the horrors of the past are openly displayed. When you visit Strokestown House and Park you see only beauty, pictures, landscape, interesting objects and wonderful old furniture.
>
> But in the minds of old people, who are now free to roam about this once private place, there lives the sad and frightening memories of their fathers', grandfathers', and great grand-fathers' suffering under the rule of the Mahons and the Packenhams of Strokestown.

Dodd recalls that Olive Hales Packenham-Mahon's grandson, Hugh, was outraged by David's speech that day. He took exception, unreasonably, according to Dodd, with David's train of thought and references to the family's legacy in Roscommon, though David had spoken sympathetically about the family's last days in the great house. 'Who is this David Thomson, is he some sort of socialist or communist?' he asked afterwards. Dodd says the man failed to see the subtleties of what David was saying. And he might have been confused by the writer's accent being so like his own.

Thomson had also pointed out that in the late eighteenth century Thomas Mahon of Strokestown, a member of the Irish Parliament, strongly opposed the Act of Union. He was one of the Protestant gentry who fought against the dissolution, which was achieved partly through bribery. Olive Hales Packenham-Mahon, the last Anglo-Irish resident of the house, had recalled this history with sympathy to David many years before. Her family history and recollections of that bygone era also featured in the work of Jim Fahy of RTÉ in his radio series, 'Looking West'. Nicholas, her son, who died in 2012, was the last link with the Strokestown House of old, and he had kept in contact over the years with the house's new owner, Jim Callery, a local businessman.

Strokestown House, County Roscommon (courtesy Strokestown Park and the National Famine Museum).

Thomson's speech includes a semantic note, when he took issue with the terms 'Ulster' and 'Northern Ireland', and suggested that the term 'Six Counties', though unacceptable even to people of moderate views, was, in fact, more accurate. Then he said that the Packenham-Mahons were lucky to live in the beautiful county of Roscommon:

> Perhaps I'm sentimental because it is the only county in Ireland I know intimately, every mile, every town, fair days in many towns, villages, hills, lakes and mountains belong to my youth. I regard the county as my Alma Mater, my gentle mother – just as I regard the whole of Ireland as my adopted country.
>
> I want to leave, as my last words here, my very best wishes to the place and everyone concerned with it.

David also recorded an interview on location at Woodbrook House with Joe Mulholland of RTÉ. Joe's purpose was to record David's reflections, as a possible background piece to the Jennifer Johnston *Woodbrook* drama that was in development at the time, but which, for various reasons, never materialized.

David's deteriorating hearing meant that the questions frequently had to be repeated. He was coughing, his speech was halting and he tended to lose his train of thought. The erudition and sense of detail in *Woodbrook* or *Nairn* seem far away.

Less than a year later, in an obituary, Seamus Heaney described David's end of life frailty candidly but joyfully: 'His body may have demeaned him in the end with hearing troubles, eyesight problems and unsteadiness of limb but it also served him well as the instrument of delight. It expressed with great suppleness and alacrity his gleefulness and his sudden humorous illuminations.'

And as the RTÉ camera rolled that July day in 1987, despite his frailty, there were still interesting reflections in David's mind. He recalled the advantage of savouring the countryside in his Woodbrook years, cycling or on horseback: 'I think I had an intimate knowledge of North Roscommon at that time – in that way – and I now think that it was a rather valuable foundation – of one's imagination and one's experience of life, colours, colours of the landscape and movement of cloud, animals, people ... I value it anyway.'

He again recalled Phoebe and what he called her 'agility'. This was the last recollection of the great love affair, in the house where it grew so strongly, over fifty years before:

> In Scotland we call it – and it's a lovely word – jimp. 'Jimp' means slender, agile, graceful in movement. She was that, you see. I think it is in her movement ... her body was very beautiful, either dancing or on horse. People on horses can look ... clumsy, puddingly, but she ... she was so mobile, so responsive to the horse and that's what a good rider should be – almost like part of the horse. Bicycling too, though it may sound strange, it was that. I loved to watch her on a bicycle. If she went ahead of me it's a beautiful picture I have of her in my mind, yes.

The Packenham-Mahon family in 1900. The child in the picture is Olive, then aged six. On her left is her mother, May Burrard. Next to her is her father, Henry Packenham-Mahon, who apparently took the photo using a timer (courtesy Strokestown Park and the National Famine Museum).

David Thomson at Woodbrook House, July 1987 (© RTÉ Archives).

He recalled also, as he stood in the then derelict stable yard, the dances that were held every year close to or on the date of Phoebe's birthday, 12 September. What remained of the timbers of the upper floor were then open to the sky, where he and others had once carefully cleared the oats away in sacks and spread soap flakes on the wood to transform it into a ballroom – of sorts. He said he was never great as a dancer, but could only walk now with the aid of a stick as he recalled those distant nights.

In September 1987 the Thomsons went to Provence for a holiday. Martina was the diarist this time. She describes, with a painter's eye, 'the valleys misty in the mornings, the outline of the hills faint and blue in the distance'. She saw to the south the faintest outline of Cézanne's Mont Saint Victoire. 'Such grandeur, would I could hold it in my heart?'

Perhaps in writing these words she was realizing that she could not hold on forever to her life with David.

17. Nairn in Light

In early 1987 the Conservative Party chairman and MP, Norman Tebbit, discussed the virtue of increasing numbers of people becoming company shareholders. David Thomson took him to task:

> It is true that Britain is becoming a nation of shareholders. Napoleon called England a nation of shopkeepers – same thing! It is also true and the boost to business you are proud of confirms it – that it is a nation of millions of unemployed and homeless people. This is one of the achievements of the Conservative Party.

In December, David was named the McVitie Scottish Writer of the Year for *Nairn in Darkness and Light*. This award was a kind of coming full circle, a recognition towards the end of his life for a work that eloquently expressed his childhood years. He and Martina travelled north to receive the award in Abbotsford, the home of Sir Walter Scott, on the banks of the Tweed. Martina's diary describes the journey through Lancashire: 'We drove up a dark blue road, over a russet orange stretch of hills to the Yarrow Valley.'

David was so happy to be in Abbotsford, among Sir Walter Scott's things. He had recently reread *Guy Mannering*, Scott's hugely popular novel published in 1815. Edinburgh's central station, Waverley, takes its name from the writer's earlier historical novel. Martina discovered that Scott and David shared a similar childhood; both were injured and taken from the city to grow up with relatives in the country, where, she says, 'both claimed an unusual freedom'.

Nairn in Darkness and Light has, as one of its themes, the freedom of thought, and inspiration that knowledge creates. David took to learning so eagerly, because it stimulated him so much. A retired teacher who lived nearby in Nairn, Mr Rae, was appointed the young Thomson's tutor. He 'stretched my intellect and emotions far beyond the limits that my previous teachers had set'. Literature came first in their relationship. There was a great local connection: only four miles from Nairn is Cawdor Castle – King Duncan's castle in *Macbeth* in the foothills of the Grampian Mountains. They studied the classics – nearly a year, he says, on *Moby-Dick* and another on *Les Misérables*. When David told him he had finished *The Mill on the Floss* 'he plunged me into *Middlemarch*'. Mr Rae gave an incidental lesson to the future writer on narrative structure when, reading aloud, he broke off at a moment of suspense to make his pupil long for their next meeting.

Their engagement with history was just as productive. Mr Rae (Thomson doesn't refer to his first name) began one lesson with: 'Tell me Thomson, of some important happenings in your own life?' David mentioned his kick in the head, the slaughter of the hens, his Uncle Tom falling down the Newton stairs. He couldn't remember dates. Mr Rae said the main thing was that he had peopled the events:

> The study of history can be like your own memory, in a jumble. Any happening that interests you can be studied first. Dates are important only if one happening is the consequence of another. It is probably better to start with the history of a place you know well than to struggle with the history of Tibet. The Battle of Culloden is distant in time but near this room in place.

One of Thomson's legacies is this advocacy, found throughout his writing, of the value of knowledge. A former *Guardian* correspondent, Neil Ascherson, referred to this when enthusing about *Nairn* in the *London Review of Books*: 'This book should be on the reading list of all ambitious courses in the literature and social history of Scotland. David Thomson, his senses sharpened by poor sight, managed to absorb the way that *Nairn in Darkness and Light* "worked".'

The harbour at Nairn.

David, towards the end of his life, was attracted again to Scotland. Nairn inspired his last work which he never completed. 'Sandstorm' is based on a celebrated climatic event near Nairn in 1694 that smothered the village of Cublin. David remembered the area and its sand dunes in *Nairn*, where the family would picnic, as a mysterious place. His father once told him that when the wind shifts the sand things can turn up: 'You might trip over the church steeple,' he warned, adding to the mystery.

'Flood' is set in the aftermath of another famous storm of August 1829. It's what he called a film-play, something he hadn't attempted before, and included suggested camera shots. It's a period piece dealing with laird-tenant relationships against the background of the devastating floods on the Nairn and Findhorn rivers. He had begun both works in 1986 and was pleased with his progress, Martina recalled in 2013.

His bolder side, the David Thomson of the African adventures, is also evident in a section of a 1987 notebook, titled 'Notes for a Fanny Hill of the 1980s', in which he examines the tradition of flagellation and observes that 'people flogging themselves in religious processions seem to be a disguised form of sexual satisfaction'. It would have been fascinating to see how this project had turned out.

Bridge over the River Nairn from which Martina Thomson scattered David's ashes on 12 October 1988.

David Thomson noted in his diary on 8 January 1988 that he was writing an obituary for Terence Tiller, his BBC colleague: 'But I am 74, he was 72.' David himself was to die within two months. He opened his obituary for his friend with words from John Donne: 'When she the Church buries a man, that action concerns me; All mankinde is of one Author and is one Volume; when one man dies, one Chapter is not torne out of the Booke …'

One day a piercing pain convulsed David as he attempted to load the kitchen range, a job he always undertook. It was late January 1988. He hadn't been feeling well for a while and had seen a doctor. Martina contacted the doctor again, mentioning this incident, and he rewrote the referral letter for David to a consultant. David's pallor was quite yellow and he had very little strength, she recalled. It was serious. In hospital they did investigatory surgery, and the news wasn't good. David had cancer of the oesophagus. A second operation was suggested, but David wasn't keen and opted to leave hospital. He was very weak.

Martina recalls something that happened at this time. They were in their old haunt, The Edinburgh Castle, one afternoon. Beryl Bainbridge was there. David wanted to talk to her, but when he approached, she ignored him.

When Bainbridge wrote after David's death expressing her condolences, Martina couldn't resist asking in her reply why she had ignored him that day?

It was because his bad hearing made conversation difficult, Bainbridge said. On that occasion at least, she wasn't, it seems, prepared to make the effort. 'It was rotten,' Martina said. 'But then one of his more down and out acquaintances sat down next to him and that was good.'

David's seventy-fourth birthday was on the 17 February. He was getting weaker when the Thomsons decided on a weekend away, and Martina drove them to the White Lion Hotel in Aldeburgh in Suffolk, a coastal town with a famous shingle beach and associated with the composer, Benjamin Britten. It was a special offer weekend in the hotel. David became ill the first night, 23 February, and Martina sent for a doctor and David was given morphine. He had only days to live.

Only Martina was told how ill he was. So they didn't discuss death or make requests or wishes. It was a sombre time; their receipt shows a mere £2 spent in the bar, during their three-night stay. Ben Thomson gave his father an Indian hare ornament as a birthday present. David decided to found the Society of the Hare there and then, writing down the names of the members and putting them in the ornament, which opened into a small box; the names were Ben, Martina, Seamus Heaney, Marie Heaney and David himself. The wooden hare remained on David's desk until the family home was sold in 2014.

The wooden hare given to David by his son, Ben,
for what was his last birthday, 17 February 1988.

He was moved to the Cottage Hospital. Martina slept on the floor beside him. They had only four more days together. Martina recorded that period in her diary a month later: 'It took a little while for the injection to work – you were desperate now, but I was able to calm you, told you to breathe deeply

– in, out, breathing with you and stroking you. You were grateful for this and clutched my hand strongly. In, out and gradually you became calmer …'

Luke Thomson recalls being shocked when he saw his father. He hadn't been home for a while, as he was married and living in France: 'I actually spent a lot of time with him then, just talking. He held my hand and kept telling me his dreams. He was attending his own funeral.'

The morphine doses gave David one last great high, Martina recalls. He 'demanded' a taxi to take him into town. He talked all the time, Martina wrote in her diary later: 'His sentences started loud and clear, but faded and did not seem to connect, but almost did. One did: My mind is so funny … it can't remember the natural world, so it continues to search for an impossible world.'

Then he had a quiet day. The hospital suggested to Martina that she get a room nearby, which she did, but it was never used. She stayed by the bedside, with their three boys. David died that night, 27 February 1988.

In his notebook there's an appointment for the following Monday, the launch of the paperback edition of *Nairn*. The rest of this 1988 notebook, given to him the previous Christmas by Martina, is empty, apart from one note he had written for 1 March – 'cancel gardening mag'. David received a posthumous prize later that year for *Nairn in Darkness and Light*, the inaugural NCR Award for Non Fiction, beating Claire Tomalin, Michael Ignatieff and Max Hastings, among others.

In *The Listener* of 24 March 1988 Frank Delaney recalled a card he'd received from David just before his death, with its 'large black handwriting, like the strides of a bird across the paper'.

Delaney was reviewing a season of Tennessee Williams plays he'd seen the previous week in the National Theatre. Was there a connection, he wondered, between a chronicler of the Deep South and one of the 'fading Gaelic islands', as Delaney called them? Yes, he thought: 'With *Woodbrook* and *Nairn in Darkness and Light*, David Thomson showed his expertise with a unique brand of topographic writing, where history and personal experience merged to give not only a sense of place, but also a feeling of time.'

The Daily Telegraph said he was a 'sensitive master of nostalgic evocation'. The historian Roy Foster wrote in *The Irish Times*: 'It is a terrible wrench to think of passing Regent's Park Terrace and not to see that frail head with its green eyeshade and blue French cap bent laboriously over his desk. But the books he wrote there and in Edingthorpe will endure, and so will his indomitable spirit.'

David Thomson had been a writer, a radio producer, a folklorist and historian. He had passion and humanity. He was brilliant and he was honest. But it was Seamus Heaney who best captured a sense of both the artist and the person.

> He had, in Yeats's words, 'something to perfection brought'. As a writer he succeeded in giving form not only to much that he cherished, but also to much that he had lost.
>
> There was about him a delicate wildness, and he often thought that the hare, about which he had gathered so many entrancing stories, was his proper totem animal. Shy vivid and capable of swift epiphanies.*

* *The Independent*, 2 March 1988.

Postscript

In 2012 Martina Thomson was diagnosed with spinal cancer. She fought the disease, living independently until close to her death on 23 September 2013. On the day of her funeral service in Golders Green Crematorium on 3 October, Ben Thomson recalled something that happened during her final days. She hadn't been eating and was eventually persuaded to try the hospital food. The story is an echo of happier times when the family holidayed near Lough Key in 1968 as David was researching *Woodbrook*. The landlady was serving dinner one day to Martina and the boys, and the vegetable was turnip. Ben, then eight, said, 'I don't like turnip.' He was told that it was not turnip – it was swede. 'Whatever it is I don't like it,' said the young Thomson. Now, as Martina attempted the same vegetable from the hospital menu and so weak she could barely speak, she recalled this old family story and said to Ben, 'Whatever it is, I don't like it.'

Her ashes were scattered, as she had scattered David's, on the waters of the Nairn River.

Martina Thomson's Diary

April 1988, Camden

You came home week after week with flowers for me, bought preferably at the corner stall. Sometimes they made me sad – I wished to paint them and succeeded so rarely. Now I carry home flowers to place on your desk. I walk up Parkway with my bunch. Your bringing me flowers implied my bringing them for you. By the symmetry of our acts I am deluded and feel you take part in this. I walk as if towards you.

Index